Praise for Football Flyboy

Football Flyboy *is a story with earthiness and honesty we have largely forgotten today, punctuated with the heartsick loneliness that only a soldier out of contact with his family for extended periods can understand. Each chapter opens with "one of the letter" and closes with the author's Aunt Ruby's poems—highlighting the point of the chapter or just providing the reader with a smile or a tear. An entertaining read and not a typical War story.*

—**Bob P.,** former tinker, soldier, sailor, spy

Bravo to an ordinary man who had the desire to be the best version of himself, regardless of his circumstances and the challenges of war. Through the eyes of his daughter comes First Lt William R Cannon, United States Army Air Force story on the rich history of the WWII era and his flight around the world. I found myself laughing out loud at his unique humor and didn't want the story to end. Fly away with Football Flyboy! *I would have been honored to have known and served with him.*

—**Andi Sue Phillips,** United States Naval Aviator

Holy Cow, I don't know where to start but Football Flyboy *had me on an emotional roller coaster. One minute I'm trying not to laugh out loud and the next I'm trying not to cry. I'm sitting here in my office trying not to cry as I tell you how much I enjoyed this story, yet tears are rolling down my face.*

You are sharing other's stories and at the same time, you are giving little history lessons. I loved how you wrote this jumping back and forth from Buster's letters to the family stories, to history about that time and your take on everything. Football Flyboy reminds me of the show "This is Us."

There is so much in this book that it isn't just one genre. It's a love story, it's a history book, it's a memoir, and it's a biography of parts of your life. My point is: you made me feel a ton of emotions as I read this and I love it.

—**Mariah Trujillo,** publisist

Football Flyboy

First Lt. Bill Cannon,
Piloting More than
His Own Aircraft

Lisa Reinicke

Our House Publications

Our House Publications
Copyright 2018 by Our House Publications
All rights reserved.

No part of this book may be reproduced in any written, electronic, recording or photocopying without the written permission from the publisher or author. The exception would be in the case of brief quotations embodied in the critical articles and reviews and pages where permission is specifically granted by the publisher or author.

Although every precaution has been taken to verify the accuracy of the information contained herein, the author and publisher assume no responsibility for any errors or omissions. No liability is assumed for damages that may result from the use of information contained within.

Edited by Judith Briles and John Mathewson
Cover and interior design by Rebecca Finkel, F + P Graphic Design
Judith Briles, The Book Sheperd

Library of Congress Control Number: 2018932152
Hard cover 978-0-9993637-3-7
Trade paper 978-0-9993637-4-4
ebook 978-0-9993637-5-1

To order bulk sales for organizations and schools contact Kayla@LisaReinicke.com

Other books by Lisa Reinicke and Our House Publications
Bart's Escape, Arnold, the Cute Little Pig with Personality, David's Christmas Wish, and **Wings and Feet.**
Visit us at www.LisaReinicke.com or www.OurHousePublications.com

Printed in USA

Dedications and Acknowledgements

First, this is to my mom for saving all of these letters and allowing me to be part of my parent's intimate life. Thank you to our Flyboy, for showing us that our circumstances should never be an excuse for our actions. We are the pilots of our own aircraft in life.

To all the families who think theirs is crazy and become estranged, I hope this book helps you to embrace those crazies and love them where they are. I love you all my family for building me from a baby to whom I am today. You each added fiber to my construction.

The people in this book leave us an example and footprints we can follow. It was a journey of listening to the past, and it has changed my future. My greatest hope is that in reading this story, it will inspire the reader to examine life for meaning and the gifts they will leave on earth.

Thank you to my family for putting up with my obsession to complete this book and allowing me to envelope myself into the past. I am delighted to leave you all with the heritage this story brings.

Thanks to Judith for taking me under your wing, editing, providing guidance, and the courage to dive in to write a novel. Your tutoring kept me going. Your editing made the book come together yet you left the integrity of the story intact. You spent many, many hours poring over manuscripts. It is appreciated.

John for initial edits and letting me bounce all of past, present, and poetry off of you. Your honesty as each chapter finished helped me to complete a sentence structure and spelling that made sense when my ideas went wildly off topic. You fit me into your spare time, which I know you didn't have.

Mariah thanks for your patience and creativity. You are a right and left arm to me, and sometimes my brain. You kept me focused and on track so that I could complete this book.

I don't want to leave out Kayla for promoting my work and reaching beyond your comfort zone to get these books into events and stores.

Last but not least Rebecca for making this a beautiful work of art. You are a rockstar. The words were raw before you put it all together. I threw you a bunch of paint, and you made a masterpiece.

I am truly blessed and thank the Lord above for placing me in this family, or this story would be entirely different. This family chose me and made me. They loved me and taught me how to love others especially those who appear unlovable.

Contents

PREFACE: Words 7
CHAPTER 1: Leaving Home 11
CHAPTER 2: The Best Child........................... 17
CHAPTER 3: Bill 23
CHAPTER 4: The Goose.................................. 29
CHAPTER 5: Atomic Bomb............................ 33
CHAPTER 6: The Mink Coat 37
CHAPTER 7: Sondrestrom Air Base, Greenland..... 41
CHAPTER 8: Still No Mail 47
CHAPTER 9: Vinegar on French Fries................ 51
CHAPTER 10: Sitting on My Fanny 55
CHAPTER 11: War Can Make Everyone Act Ugly.... 59
CHAPTER 12: The Three Day Tour 63
CHAPTER 13: Silk Pajamas............................... 73
CHAPTER 14: Happiest People 79
CHAPTER 15: Movies...................................... 83
CHAPTER 16: Jabbering 89
CHAPTER 17: Slow Screws 95
CHAPTER 18: Hope of Mail............................. 99
CHAPTER 19: They Are Humans..................... 107
CHAPTER 20: Mail... 109

CHAPTER 21: Leaving Shanghai	115
CHAPTER 22: Command Performance	119
CHAPTER 23: Demons	125
CHAPTER 24: Going to the Chapel	131
CHAPTER 25: Not Pamela Sue	137
CHAPTER 26: No Letters Today	145
CHAPTER 27: Not and Excuse	149
CHAPTER 28: In the Gutter	155
CHAPTER 29: Flunky	159
CHAPTER 30: No Commentary Needed	165
CHAPTER 31: Japs to Dinner	171
CHAPTER 32: Done Is Done	177
CHAPTER 33: It Doesn't Seem Like Christmas	183
CHAPTER 34: Coming Home	189
CHAPTER 35: They Got It All	193
CHAPTER 36: The Heart Knows	197
CHAPTER 37: You Eat It	201
CHAPTER 38: Hurry	205
CHAPTER 39: Last Letter	209
Afterword	215
Cannon Recipes	217
About the Author	222

PREFACE

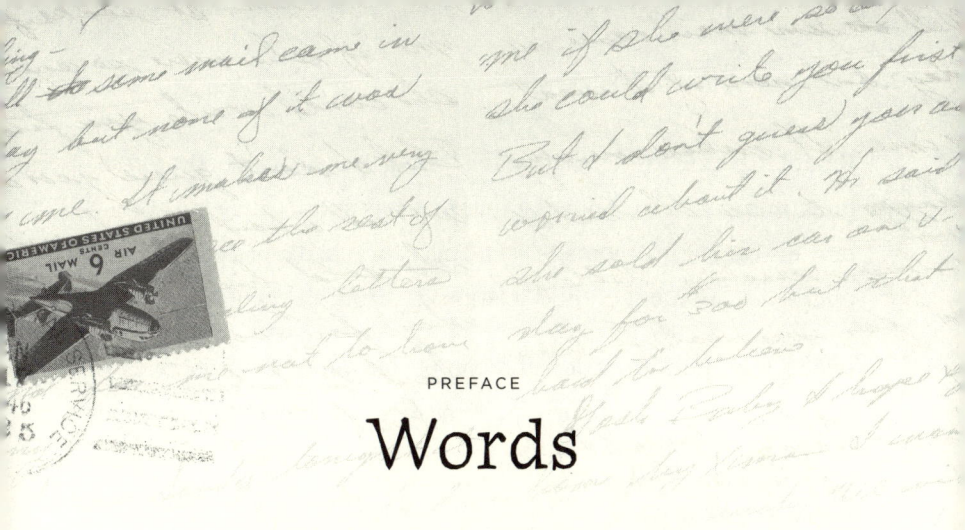

Words

*Before reaching inside, there was a feeling
of the hands of time grabbing onto my heart ...*

A good man's life cannot end at his death. His deeds, no matter how small, get passed down for many generations. His spirit does not stay silent just because his mouth can no longer speak words.

What does it take to be a good man? What are the right ingredients? How much honor, laughter, tears, and commitment are just enough? Can a good man have done bad things and then be changed? The measurement of a good man is that he has value. Each passion of his life builds him into a man of worth until his death.

Little did I know, I was about to embark on a journey that would redefine my father and let me see how his personal experiences accumulated to reveal his wisdom.

I open my dad's old air force footlocker—still solid, battleship grey, weathered, and a little rough from travel and age. His name is in white lettering on the front: **First Lt William R Cannon**.

Before reaching inside, there was a feeling of the hands of time grabbing onto my heart, knowing that this was such a huge part of not only his life but my mom's as well. This period had a profound impact on the development of their relationship from the beginning.

Inside was the foundation that supported more than 55 years of marriage. The souls of my parents rose up and spoke as pages unfolded from his envelopes. Their voice was of two young newlyweds kept apart by war, yet so close and so real was their relationship.

> **These were times that human bonds went far beyond superficial conversation ...**

I would see their personal feelings and share in their loneliness, sorrows, joy, and adventures through the love letters inside which told their story.

The letters demonstrate they took their vows seriously. They contain family secrets, unselfishness, tenderness, and love; the kind that death could not steal.

The letters are a one-sided conversation of a man who lived for someone more important than himself. The struggles of war kept him from receiving mail regularly, causing frustration and loneliness.

These were times that human bonds went far beyond superficial conversation, and the small snippets we now share about ourselves through social media. The roots sought great depths and reached great lengths. Words took hold and kept relationships together.

This age took courage and commitment. It was a time that was not filled with instant gratification or instant anything for that matter. Human relationships were held tightly with a determination not to give up. To give up would be too high a cost.

PREFACE: Words

So, I reached in and took the first pile of fragile, yellowed envelopes held together with twine. Now, jumping into a story of long before I came to be, I began swimming in the sea of precious words. I wish I had known the story before my parents were gone but it is doubtful that I could have appreciated it then. If only we could be wiser when we are younger. How much fuller would we live life and how much better it could make us? I know it would have made me a better person if I hadn't celebrated the foolishness of youth.

My dad was my hero. He was the one that I could not disappoint. Dad was wise and could read my intentions, knowing when my heart was hard or soft so he could deliver the consequences that would teach me the right lesson.

Dad was a manly man, strong, but with a laugh and a smile that he genuinely delivered without holding back. He could defuse any tense situation.

He was my mentor, teacher, father, defender, and my friend. These letters help me to see what made him that man.

You will also meet other members of my family—in particular, my Aunt Ruby. She wrote poetry, chronicling happenings within the family. I will share many of these with you.

You will notice grammar, spelling, and punctuation errors in the letters. I decided to preserve their authenticity and leave them unedited throughout.

Meet my dad, Bill "Buster" Cannon, the Football Flyboy ...

12 Buster the Football Flyboy

CHAPTER 1

Leaving Home

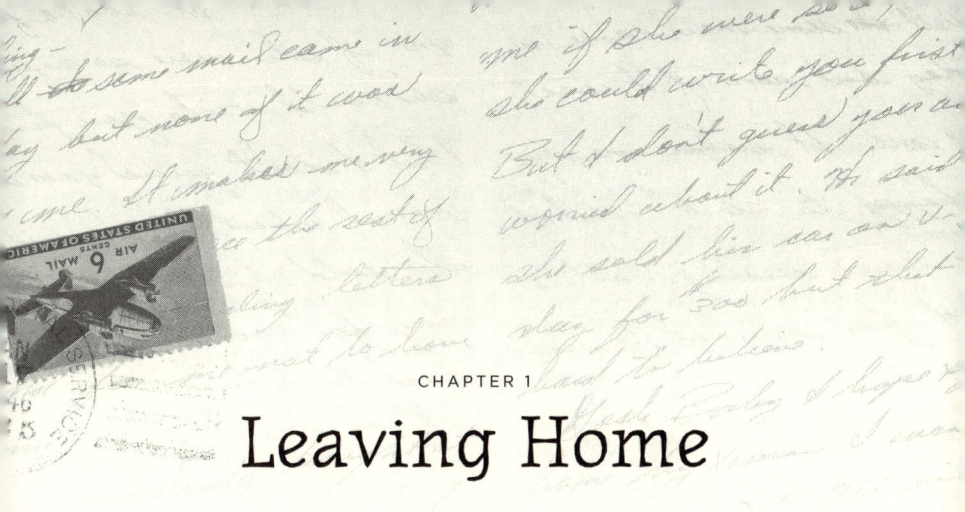

*Nothing has ever hurt me so much
as leaving home and leaving you this morning.*

August 4th, 1945

My darling wife,
First I'll tell you everything that has happened up until now. We started our engines about 20 minutes after you left and taxied out to run the engines up and take off. Well, the left engine was cutting out so we taxied back to the line and got another ship. It was five minutes to eleven before we got the other ship loaded and took off. It is better that you left when you did though because I was busy loading the other ship and couldn't have seen you.

On the way, I read two chapters of Amber and tried to sleep the rest of the way. We got here about 5 pm and I had to set my watch up to 6 because this is Eastern Time. We unloaded and were assigned barracks and drew bedding, and then we ate. We will process in the morning and then have an inspection and get our equipment tomorrow afternoon and Sunday morning we take off for Maine then our destination. I can't tell you where or what to expect. There are 30 crews of us, a total of 128 men. The 1st crews on the roster will fly the ships and the rest will go as passengers. I am so glad we fly instead of going by boat.

Darling, I can't begin to tell you how brave you were this morning. I'm so glad you didn't break down and cry because I would have too. Nothing has ever hurt me so much as leaving home and leaving you this morning. I know I'll cry tonight but I don't care. I am glad I have Amber to keep me company. If I didn't have her to read I would go nuts but I still can't concentrate on her for thinking of you.

I will send you a wire tomorrow and will try to call if I have time. I hope I can reach you by phone tomorrow because if I don't I will have no way of knowing if you got home safely. I hope so much that you didn't have any trouble.

When you write, be sure to tell me when you left Austin and every single detail of your trip. Honey it was sort of nice that Sandy and Dorothy were with us because we both may have been crying our eyes out if we had been alone.

Darling, I've got to go now and cry myself to sleep. You always remember that I love you so very, very much and I miss you more than words can ever tell.

Always thinking of you, Buster

A GOOD MAN will open up and be honest about his feelings. Dad was so venerable in this letter. He opened his gut and spilled out the pain of having to leave his new bride standing there. He worried because he did not know if his wife got home OK or not.

Dad wasn't ashamed that he was going to cry himself to sleep. He wanted Mom to know it was hurting him as much as it was hurting her that they were going to be apart for so long. I never saw my dad cry. He saved that as a private revelation with my mom.

A good man is one that has compassion. He can laugh and cry. He faces eternity and isn't afraid to die.

A good man will fight for honor.

We all can relate to the hurt of saying goodbye to someone we love. For me, this letter brings back memories of when we took our oldest son to Marine Corps boot camp, and later our youngest son to serve in a Marine Corps tour in Iraq. I held it together while saying goodbye with hugs, smiles, and encouragement. When out of sight, the tears burst and I made that grotesque face. The face you make when you turn your mouth inside out, and your eyes squeeze tight in your sorrow. You get that ugly cry face that is much more than a cry; it becomes a wailing that is inside trapped deep within your soul. No sound comes out. No tears stream down because the anguish is stuck and will not leave.

Our youngest son, Steve, was going overseas right at the height of the Iraq conflict. The news played on every channel, and I can remember watching *CNN* consistently to see what was going on, thinking I might get a chance to see him on camera. If I just watched close enough, there might be a chance that I would get a glance of him. It would assure me to know he was OK. For Mom and Dad, their war was one of secrets.

Their war was one of secrets.

I think about how tough Mom was to keep it together and not cry until all backs were turned then break down, which I know she had to have done. Hers would be the ugly face of tears after he could not see her. She did not know where in the world her loved one was going and even when he knew; he might not be able to tell her.

Theirs was a war of silent suffering and waiting. There were no cell phones, no satellite phones, and no email. Communication was only through letters that took long to reach each other. It had to have been agonizing.

Our son, Steve, had the modern convenience of email available to him. He was even allowed to use his sergeant's satellite phone on certain occasions. One such event was when his unit was in need of toilet paper!

In the field, they lived mostly on Meals Ready to Eat (MREs), and there was a little tiny square of toilet paper in the MRE; their allotment for the day. Even though a poop was hard to come by after eating nothing but constipating MREs, the guys needed toilet paper.

I was the Marine's mom. It was my mission to make sure these young men were well stocked. Donations came from churches, schools, and neighborhoods, supplying our guys with a multitude of goodies.

There would be jerky, which the guys loved, and homemade cookies. Steve said the cookies were as if they were fresh out of the oven. It was so hot where they were that packages reached more than 100 degrees when they arrived. We tried sending gum, but he said it arrived so gooey that it looked like it had already been chewed. "Don't send gum, Mom!"

Around all the goodies, I would pad the box with toilet paper. It had enough for all the men on every base, and it was the coveted Charmin brand.

When the boxes would not arrive for a few days, Steve's sergeant would ask him, "Reinicke, how long since you've phoned home?" Then he would toss him the satellite phone to call me to ask for more toilet paper.

I looked up the novel *Forever Amber* that Dad was talking about in the same letters. It didn't surprise me that it was a little naughty. It was about an abandoned, pregnant, and penniless sixteen-year-old Amber living on the streets of London. She uses her wits, beauty, and courage to climb to the status of the favorite mistress of the Merry Monarch, Charles II. She remains faithful to the one man she loves, the one man she can never have.

Amber wasn't a book that you would expect a manly man to read, but then Dad was full of surprises.

As I became an adult, I started reading my mom's books once she finished them. They were all a little naughty. In fact, the first book my mother gave me, she had taken a black sharpie and marked through all the naughty parts so I could not read them. Here I was a grown woman reading a book that my mom had censored!

My mom and dad were sweethearts all the way back in the first grade. Their families knew each other. My parents had always been fond of one another, and dated in high school. My dad was the star football player, who also carried a football star attitude. My mom, a proper lady, was a drama poetry reader.

Growing up my mom would still recite poetry to me, cute little snippets here and there. I still remember many of them and have repeated them to my children and now my grandchildren. One of my favorites is an old English nursery rhyme.

Little Fly Upon the Wall
Little fly upon the wall
Ain't you got no clothes at all?
Ain't you got no pettiskirt?
Ain't you got no undershirt?
Gee little fly ain't you cold?

There was also this one she would recite to me:

I saw a little bird go hop, hop, hop.
I said little bird won't you stop, stop, stop.
I went to the window to say "how do you do."
And he shook his little tail and away he flew.

My mom would tell me stories where my dad would leave class if the teacher didn't let my mom, Mary Jo, read the lesson for the day. Not only would Dad leave class but all his football cronies would walk out of class with him. He had the teacher bushwhacked, and he managed to embarrass mom as well.

Mom was ladylike, and Dad knew how to treat her like a lady, but on one memorable occasion however, there was an incident.

The scene was movie worthy. A handsome young man smiled and wooed the leading lady as she daintily balanced on a brick fence. When she got to the end of the wall, she jumped down into his waiting arms, but just at that moment . . . he farted. This movie became a silent film; neither one spoke the rest of the way home.

Today the lady on the fence would jump to the ground to show her agility and independence. And if either of them farted, they would think it was funny and both of them would laugh. We are definitely less inhibited today. And that's a good thing!

God didn't have to give our gas a noise or smell, but he chose to do so because He had a sense of humor. I can't help thinking about angels in heaven laughing at our farts.

Dramatic Pupils To Give Recital

Miss Mary Jo Cook

Pictured above is Miss Mary Jo Cook, young dramatic instructor, who will present her pupils in a recital at Jefferson school auditorium, Tuesday evening at 8 o'clock.

Miss Cook, who is 15 years old, is the daughter of Mr. and Mrs. John F. Cook 633 North Park street, and is a pupil of Mrs. Rhetta Mae Dorland, head of the dramatic art and speech department at Oklahoma Baptist university. The recital will be open to the public.

Ilene Ashford will act as pianist, the pupils who will appear on the program being Jackie Hohenstein, Mary Bea Renshaw, Billie Jo Poole, Jeanette Posey, Patsy Combs, Marilyn Miller, Charlene and Carolyn Randall, Virginia and Rebecca Perry, Mozelle Troxell, Tony Switzer, Bobbie Louise Owens, Mary Bell Geno, Zahaia Hassen, Betty Lorraine Deatherage, Betty Faye Wiles, Billy Jo Thomas, Nancy Jane Thomas, Joy Byrd, Pauline Poe, Leona Hall, Norma Jean Combs, Barbara Jean McGee, Betty Bailey, Darlene Neyman and Marcia Jayne Cook.

* * *

CHAPTER 2

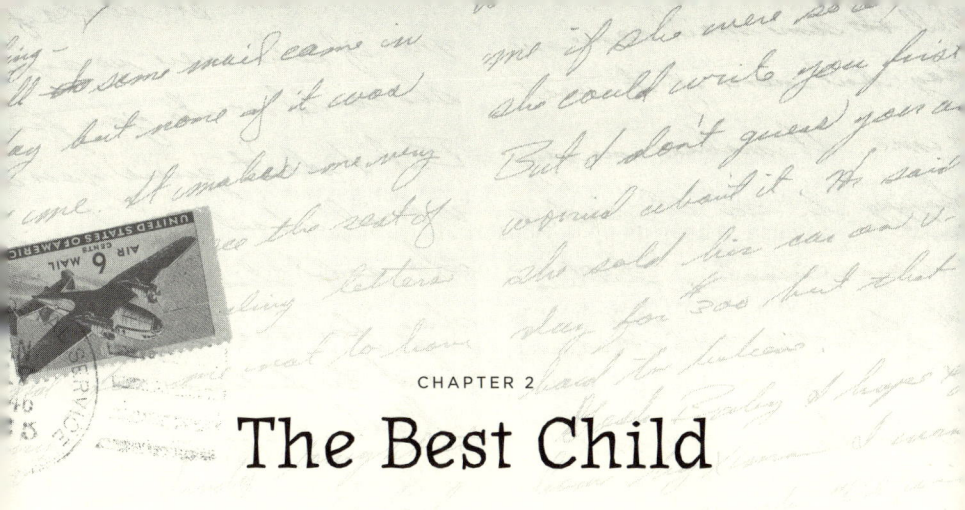

The Best Child

*From the day he was born
the whole family has been "dancing to his tune."*

August 5th, 1945

Well, Darling you sure have a tired husband. I'm so tired I even forgot how to start a letter. I guess I should start all over and do it the proper way but I'm not.

I'm so glad I got to talk to you. Your voice sounded swell. Tell Cleo I'm sorry I couldn't get John some more khaki. I told you over the phone that I'm sending my B-4 bag home with soap and Kleenex in it. You can split the soap with Cleo and Syd and keep the Kleenex for yourself. I could have bought more but I just didn't have time to get it.

We processed this morning from 8 until 11:30 and then I sent you the telegram. This afternoon we drew our equipment and had our clothes inspected The last bunch to leave from here went to Bangor Maine, Labrador, Greenland, Iceland, London, or Scotland, Paris or Southern France, Turin, Cayce, Calcutta, or Karachi.

I'm not allowed to tell you how or where we will go but the rest have gone that way so you can draw your own conclusion.

I drew an Army B-4 bag, another canvas bag, and a muster bag and a mess gear bag. There were all kinds of flying cloths and equipment. We are sending our footlockers over by water because we can't carry but 125 lbs by air. We got a new type of parachute and it is a good one. We also got our life preserver, in case to keep us up to float in the water, and a swell walk out kit with everything in it to survive if you have to crash land and have to walk out.

Darling, I have to go to bed now. I am really tired. I love you more and more each minute. And I miss you more than anything.

All my love, Buster

DAD HAD FOUR OLDER SISTERS, and my grandmother named them all very unusual names.

Cleo was the oldest and the wisest of Dad's sisters. She was very dignified and what we considered wealthy for that day; she was very much ahead of her time. She could shoot pistols and a rifle with the best of men. She usually went hunting and fishing with her husband, John, who was a big man's man. Their house had many beautiful and ornate things that were collected from all over the world, having lived in many different countries for his work in the oil business.

John was not only tall, he was stout. He also had a booming voice to match his frame. Whenever he walked into the room, you knew he was there. When children were there, he would come in the house laughing and immediately empty his pockets inside out. Lots of change would tumble out onto the floor. All the children would be on their hands and knees scrambling to pick up as much as they could.

Even when hunting Cleo was very erect and proper. John was always a gentleman, and he expected other men to be the same. On one hunting expedition, all the men were sitting around the fire cooking with shorts on, and Aunt Cleo was there with them. One of the men was sitting with his legs crossed at the knee, and his private parts were peeking out of his shorts. My Uncle John reached out with his marshmallow stick and just tapped the end of the private part, which encouraged the man to promptly get up to adjust his manly appendage.

Syd was the next in line of the girls. She was the "fun" sister that was involved with all the kids. Her name was actually Vesta Laverne, and I'm not sure how it came to be that we all came to call her Syd. That is the only name I ever heard her called.

She always wore tons of makeup. We loved going to her house because she would open up her vanity with all that makeup, and we would use every bit of it for dress up. She would also let us dress her up, and we would work for hours fixing her hair and applying her makeup.

I can still remember the smell of the makeup: it had a Merle Norman musky and waxy smell. There was pancake makeup, (the thick kind that worked into every crevice) and blush in many colors, including pink, orange, and red. The vanity also held eyeliner, mascara, lipstick, and a plethora of shadows. We would apply every one of them!

I can still hear her belly laugh when we finished because we had her made up with every color in her collection. The finale was to tease her hair as high as we could, and then spray it in place so it would not budge.

Jack Gertrude was the third sister. She was not Jackie, just Jack. I guess my grandfather wanted a boy this time.

Jack was a character whose famous line still sticks with me today when something goes wrong: "Damn, Sam." She wore high heels, drank, and smoked like a chimney until the day she died at 83. Her laugh will forever be with me.

All of Dad's sisters had the deep, throaty laugh that comes from years of smoking. (They all were a little wild and smoked one cigarette after another, which was daring for that day.) Jack was edgy, funny, likable, and sexy. She could strut and twist that bum when she walked until she was 83!

> **From the day he was born the whole family has been "dancing to his tune."**

Finally, there was Zina Renoise, the baby, who was dethroned of that title when my dad came along. She was always called "Ruby" or "Ruby Lee." I think her nickname came from her red (or ruby) hair. I also know there was always (some) jealousy that my dad took the baby's place in rank. I think that was in teasing because they did love each other, but she did resent losing what she felt was her birthright.

Siblings from home. Buster and all his sisters, from left to the right Ruby, Jack, Cleo, Dad, and Syd.

"My Brother Was an Only Child"
By Ruby Lee

From the day he was born the whole family has been "dancing to his tune." I was the only holdout! Mother used to say he was her best child. My answer to that was "of course he was because no one ever crossed him, he had his own way about everything."

The day he was born resulted in my displacement as the baby of the family and also caused my first real punishment.

It happened this way: Jack and I were sent to Mrs. Thompson's because Mother was in labor. We chased the ice wagon down the street and Jack, being older, jumped on, and I didn't make it. Of course, I fell and howled with pain and anger which brought the whole episode to attention. Mrs. Thompson made us sit on a trunk in her dining room as punishment. It seemed like forever, probably 10 minutes. We could hear celebration next door at the advent of a baby boy!

Because of my sweet, forgiving nature, I was eventually able to overcome my resentment and came to love him too, very dearly.

Most people think Bud (the name she called Dad) is a chauvinistic, right-wing, Republican. I think he's a phony! Being non-political I don't even know what a right wing Republican is, but I've heard enough to know they are unpleasant people. It occurs to me that after the disaster of the last 12 years of a Republican government that no one would claim to be a Republican unless they choose to ignore the facts.

At heart, I think Buster is a liberal Democrat and has secret respect for the Clinton's—especially Hillary!

I do believe that he is sensitive as a result of having a liberated mother and four liberated sisters that have shaped his early life.

And by the way, the only time I was ever spanked by Mother it was "Buster's fault."

Ruby, who we called Auntie Ruby, had many tales about Dad through the years. There was one where she said all the sisters paid him back for being his mother's little darling by dumping his baby carriage into the stream … with him in it.

Grandma unintentionally paid Ruby back when she was driving a buckboard wagon into town. Halfway from Little to Shawnee, Oklahoma, she hit a bump and bounced Ruby out of the back of the wagon without realizing it. Grandma drove all the way to town before she noticed that Ruby was missing. She did turn around to get Ruby, only to find her walking to town, with fire coming out of that red hair.

Dad and those wild girls managed to grow up despite their fights and squabbles. They had children of their own and chose classic names for their offspring.

My grandfather, "Old Dad" to us kids, did not approve of our given names, so he renamed all of us. He addressed us by those names all of our lives.

I was "Lady." I think this was because my mom was trying to raise me to be a lady, in spite of my tomboy preferences. My cousin Melanie was "Watermelon," because Old Dad wanted to know what kind of melon she was with the name "Melon-ie."

My red-headed cousin, Bill, was "Troubles" this was due to the fact that he was always in trouble. My other cousins were "Dismo," "Honyocker," and other strange names followed. I guess he figured if his wife could pick weird names for their children, then he could nickname his grandkids whatever he wanted to.

CHAPTER 3

Bill

He was good at having little lies of intrigue, then telling the truth later and just getting a big kick out of it. This was his final laugh on us.

August 6th

My Darling Mary,

We left Savannah Georgia this morning about eight and got here at Dow Field in Bangor Maine. I am sorry I can't tell how or where we are going but I think you already know. We will make more stops in route than we had planned and leave in the morning.

It is really cool up here. We could wear our wool uniforms tonight and be real comfortable. I will probably sleep under one or 2 blankets tonight.

The boys that flew up here yesterday saw the Statue of Liberty in NY and also the Empire State building. They said they could see the hole that the B-25 made in it when it crashed. You remember reading about it.

I wish we wouldn't leave tomorrow because they are having the state fair here now and tomorrow is horse racing day. I would sure like to go. I love a good fair and betting on the horses. I know something or two about horses.

Oh yes the reason we didn't see New York is because it was raining too hard to even see our wing tips when we passed over it.

Gee Darling, I wish I could read a letter from you but I guess it will be a long time for your letters to even catch up with me.

I have to get some sleep now.

All My Love, Bill

On Saturday, July 28, 1945, William Franklin Smith Jr. was flying a B-25 bomber on a routine mission from Bedford Army Field to Newark Airport. He asked for clearance to land but was advised of zero visibility. He proceeded anyway, then became disoriented by the fog and started turning right instead of left after passing the Chrysler building.

The B-25 crashed into the north side of the Empire State Building between the 78th and 80th floors, carving an 18-by-20-foot hole in the building. One engine shot through the South side opposite the impact and flew as far as the next block. The engine dropped 900 feet and landed on the roof of a nearby building causing a fire. The other engine and part of the landing gear plummeted down an elevator shaft. It took 40 minutes to extinguish the blaze.

Fourteen people were killed: Smith, the two others aboard the bomber (Staff Sergeant Christopher Domitrovich and Albert Perna, a Navy aviation machinist's friend hitching a ride), and eleven others in the building. Smith was not found until two days later when search crews discovered that his body had gone through an elevator shaft and fallen to the bottom.

Empire State Building Crash

Reading about an airplane striking the Empire State Building in my dad's letter was a surprise ... something that I had never known

CHAPTER 3: Bill

before. I also didn't know my dad ever went by the name Bill. I have never in my life heard my mom call him Bill. In fact, no one in the entire family referred to him by that name.

As far as I had known, Dad's name was William Ray Cannon. I learned that the entire family had long awaited a boy to enter the picture, and with four older sisters naming a boy was not going to be easy. As the story goes, each sister had been determined to name him what she wanted. There were many fights among the siblings, which resulted in no name actually being chosen.

With all the squabbling about Dad's name, his mother just chose to ignore the fact that he didn't actually have a name at all. She let all those high-spirited girls call him by the name they wanted ... and this continued all his life. One called him Bud and one called him Preacher (I have no clue why), but then this name was shortened to Preach. One called him Buck and one called him Ray. His dad called him Billy and his mother just called him Baby.

> By the time he was one, officially he had no name yet.

By the time he was one, he still had no official name. His first birthday was a big celebration and included many arguments about what to name him. It was my grandmother's idea that all the names be written down and that the first name drawn would be the baby's first name and the second name drawn would be the baby's middle name.

It was time to put a name on his birth certificate, so each person put a name on a piece of paper, folded it, and put the paper into his father's cowboy hat. Dad, as a one-year-old baby, pulled out of the hat the name that would be used on his birth certificate. This was only a formality because his feisty sisters were going to continue to call him whatever they wanted. In their minds, it didn't matter to them what anyone else named him. The name each of them chose was the best, and they were sticking to it!

Mrs. Thompson, the neighbor lady that often took care of him, called him Buster. She did this because she thought he looked like Buster Brown from the Buster Brown shoe advertisements. Buster is the name that stuck with him and was the one his friends and his mother called him by all of his life.

The meaning of the name Buster.
People with this name have a deep inner desire to lead, organize, and supervise.

People with this name tend to be a strong, powerful force to all whose lives they touch. They are capable, charismatic leaders who often undertake large endeavors with great success. They value truth, justice, and discipline.

These descriptors fit Buster to a tee. It is funny how names do match the person.

All of Dad's Air Force and Army documents, paychecks, mail, and everything else I ever had seen with a name on it, were addressed to William Ray (W. R. Cannon). It was such a surprise to us after he died and we found his official birth and death certificates. It was then that we learned his real name was actually Billy Ray Cannon.

I can hear him laughing about that from somewhere in the spirit realm. He would have thought it was so funny that we found his given name. He was good at having little lies of intrigue, then telling the truth later and getting a big kick out of it. I can see his eyes twinkle and his Andy Griffith type smile as he might say, "I saved the best surprise for last."

As stated in his letter, Dad did know a thing or two about horses and was an excellent horseman. We always had horses at Grandma's property. Every Saturday growing up, Dad took me riding. It was just him and me. I was on a horse from the time I was two.

Those Saturdays were special between father and daughter. We had time to talk while riding along side by side on the country roads—about birds, trees, how water rolls over the rocks in streams, and some important thoughts during the ride would tumble out. In Dad's wisdom, he knew that you needed to let conversation breath and some things would "just happen" if not forced. Even today the smell of horse poop will instantly make all the worries in my world disappear.

I can picture Dad on his horse in heaven—his back straight and him smiling. With the reins in his left hand and his right poised on his thigh, he's looking ready for another adventure. We will have a special adventure ride again.

Our horses were always eager to get back to the barn. I learned to hold them back to keep them from running away with me. It wasn't just the horses who were excited to get back; I would be hungry and Dad's talk about lunch made my stomach growl.

At the end of our ride, Grandma would have lunch ready for us. Her apron on, her grey hair a mess, and the best home-cooked food would be served on her metal kitchen table. There were always fresh biscuits with every meal.

As Grandma aged, she could not see well. She still made biscuits though. I was about 18, and I wanted her to teach me how to make her fabulous biscuits. She started gathering the ingredients and was busy digging into her flour canister when I saw weevils moving around in the flour.

She just kept mixing that flour as fast as her hands would go, never noticing the wiggly things. I could tell she was proud to be teaching me how to pass on the biscuit making craft.

"Umm, Grandma," I said.

"Yes, dear," she replied.

"There are weevils in the flour," I commented.

"Well, shit." She laughed and then threw out the dough.

I wonder, how many weevils we ate all those years and didn't know it?

In heaven, there will be Dad on his horse, his back straight, smiling, in command of his horse. The reins in his left hand, and his right poised on his thigh, looking ready for adventure. We will have that ride again while eating biscuits with weevils.

CHAPTER 4

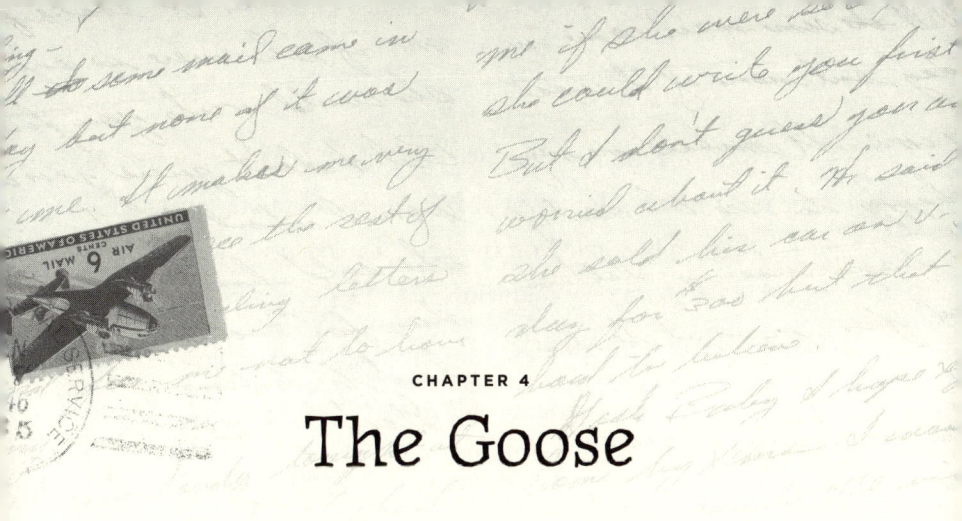

The Goose

He said they look very primitive.
I sure wish I could see some.

August 8th, 1945

Dearest Marijo

I can't write very much because in a few minutes I have to go to eat. I'm in Goose Bay in Labrador. It's pretty cool up here but not cold. It may get cold tonight though.

Besides the American Army, I've seen some Canadian civilian workers. They came here to work like your uncle did at Pearl Harbor. I haven't seen any of the natives yet but one boy said they looked awfully funny. He said they have flat faces with big boned bodies and their legs were bowed. He said they look very primitive. I sure wish I could see some.

We flew over some pretty rough terrain coming up this far and the worst is yet to come. I don't know if we will get out of here tomorrow. I would hate to stay here very long.

It was raining pretty hard only a few minutes ago but now the sun is shining. One boy is here that was supposed to leave 3 weeks ago. He needed a new tail wheel and some more parts but they haven't arrived yet.

Darling, I have to go now. I love you very, very much and I miss you more than I can say.

Bill

Goose Bay, affectionately known as "The Goose," is located in Canada's far north. More than 12,000 American military personnel and family members lived on the base. The geographical location resulted in long and very cold winters. It was not the most desirable duty.

The Innu are the Aboriginal people in Canada who live in the northeastern portion and some western portions of Labrador.

Aboriginal people of Labrador

Labrador would have been entirely a different culture for Dad to see. He would want to share that with his mom and his sisters. He passed this trait on to me. Experiencing history, different cultures, and exploring hillsides were always adventures we enjoyed together. Getting a glimpse of the Aboriginal people would have been a thrill.

Dad was curious about the world; he always wanted to see everything. He loved history, which he shared with me throughout my life. If there was a cave, he tried to explore it. If there was a battlefield, he wanted the image as it had been, and stand in the midst of it.

One trip to Gettysburg, he stood on one side of the battlefield and made me stand on the other side. "Pretend you are the Yankees, and I am the Rebels. Now fire," He yelled, as he pointed his finger at me, and we would try to reenact the drama.

"Do you see how close they would have been to each other? Can you imagine any of those men living through the Civil War?" He pondered out loud.

Dad was a lot like his mother. She traveled all over the world with her youngest daughter, Ruby, well into her 80's. Grandma had heart problems and carried nitroglycerin pills with her all the time. She didn't let health issues stop her from her explorations.

We were in New Orleans when I was young, and she had to stop to take a nitro pill and sit a spell in a transvestite club. She had a great time at the club, and she couldn't believe how beautiful the girls were. Grandma was grateful that she had to re-coop in that club because she met many lovely people. By the time she felt better, she had hugged every one of them, and they were in love with Miss Cannon.

His sisters were like that as well. Cleo traveled the world and lived in Iran, Russia, Cairo, and many other places in the U.S. She would always learn to follow the customs to live in unison with the native culture. The staff in their homes always adored Miss Cleo, but they also knew not to mess with her. They knew she ran a tight ship, and they respected that.

Miss Cleo had to have the house clean and in order at all times. In foreign countries, the vegetables needed to be washed in Clorox before eating. Clothes were required to be fresh, clean, and ironed. She taught all the servants what she expected, and they obliged knowing that Miss Cleo was tough but fair. Her generosity would spill over to the ones she was fond of.

Ruby traveled in her mind—writing stories and poetry. Her mind was always full of words. She traveled with Grandma late in life and was her best friend. It was Ruby who moved in and took care of Grandma when she got old.

Ruby even wrote a steamy romance novel that embarrassed me to read. She was terribly overweight and used to say there was a skinny girl inside of her begging to get out. Evidently, that skinny girl came out in the novel.

Jack, the rebel sister, was always off to somewhere. She would get a hair up her butt and move to Las Vegas, or somewhere else by herself. She wasn't afraid to go anywhere and had a knack for getting to know everyone around her. Neither Jack nor any of the Cannons ever met a stranger. They talked to everyone and anyone they happened to encounter.

Jack was sassy. She broke all the rules. When she had grandchildren, anything would go. If they were hungry at midnight, she would load them up in the car to go to McDonald's.

However, with her own child Gary, she was very strict. Grandma had made a chocolate cake, from scratch of course. The icing on the cake was the best part. Made with butter, cocoa, canned milk, and lots of sugar cooked on the stove to thicken and poured over the cake while it was hot. The icing would cool into a fudge topping that was to die for.

Gary was served his cake and ate only the icing off of it. "Well, I'll be damned," Jack said. "I'll just save this piece for him later," and that she did. She served it to him that evening when he wanted more cake. With a straight face and no words, Gary ate the cake.

Syd was always willing to try a new adventure. She would try anything—laughing the entire time. She pulled trailers, hauled horses, drove boats, and sat cross-legged like a man—even while wearing a dress. Those girls were feminists before their time, and so was Grandma. None of them let being a woman dictate what they could or could not do.

Syd lived the closest to Grandma so it was a daily affair that Grandma would drive by Syd's house to go to town. There was a telephone pole on the side of Syd's driveway, and Grandma ran into and knocked down that telephone pole a dozen times. Syd would always laugh about this and the fact that Grandma sat so low in her car that you couldn't see her head. Syd would say, "I saw Mother's car drive by today but not Mother."

CHAPTER 5

Atomic Bomb

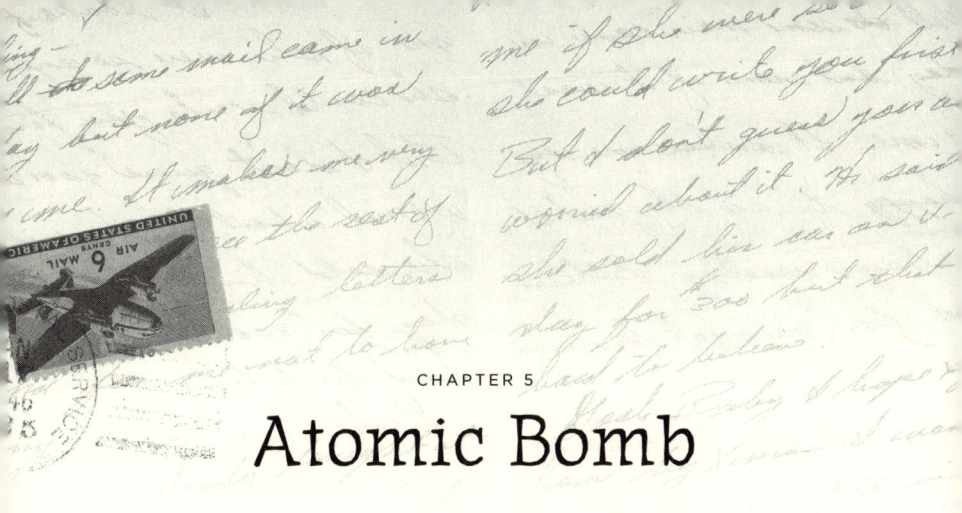

*For most people,
Dad was a defender for the underdog.*

August 9th, 1945 Labrador

Dearest Marijo,

My darling it has been terribly lonesome without you but from the looks of things it won't be long until this war is over. That new atomic bomb is really something! They dropped two of them now on Japan and they killed 150,000 people and cleared 4 square miles. I can't say I am sorry that they dropped the bomb because it will end this mess after the terrible things that have been done. Maybe I won't be gone as long as we thought.

Not that I like the bombs killing people but what the Japs have done has to be stopped. The people they are killing have to be defended. What they have done is evil.

We are weathered-in up here. This base is pretty nice. They have a nice club here and a nice hotel for colonels on up to 5 star generals and foreign diplomats of course there isn't a town near here. There are only 2 months of the year that it doesn't snow and this is one of them.

There is snow 200 miles north of here now and next stop is Greenland which is 700 miles north. Then Iceland and then like I had told you I'm liable to freeze when we hit Greenland. I would sure hate to be stationed here.

The permanent military here is pretty snotty too and I don't know why but they won't even sell us anything in the PX. I don't think they like us flyboys.

I really enjoyed my sleep last night. Maybe this war will be over soon.

Be sure to write and tell me everything that has been going on at home.

All my love, Bill

THE ATOMIC BOMB dropped on Nagasaki.

On August 9, 1945, a second atomic bomb was dropped on Nagasaki, Japan by the United States, resulting in Japan's unconditional surrender. Sadly, the devastation at Hiroshima was not sufficient to convince the Japanese War Council to accept the Potsdam Conference's demand for unconditional surrender.

> That new atomic bomb is really something.

The United States had already planned to drop its second atomic bomb, nicknamed "Fat Boy," on August 11 in the event of such recalcitrance, but the bad weather expected for that day pushed the date up to August 9. So at 1:56 a.m., a specially adapted B-29 bomber, called "Bock's Car," set out for destruction. Fat Boy was dropped at 11:02 a.m. The explosion unleashed the equivalent force of 22,000 tons of TNT. The number killed is estimated at anywhere between 60,000 and 80,000 people.

The Atomic Bomb

One has to wonder what the result of war would be today if America and the world were in the same situation as in the years between 1941 to 1945. But then, maybe we are in a similar position. The attack on the World Trade Center on 9/11 killed 2,996 people. The bombing of Pearl Harbor killed 2,403.

Similar destruction of human lives has happened in foreign lands just as it happened in Japan. It was called the Asian Holocaust, and the Japanese killed between 3,000,000 and 14,000,000 civilians and prisoners. And then think about some 207,000 Syrians, 23,000 of that number being children, and countless others whose lives have been cut down.

I sleep better knowing that we refrain from using an atomic bomb, but what will it take to stop the inhumanity? Maybe it won't stop until we are all obliterated.

The father I knew growing up believed that having compassion is better than turning away, and that not all people from any nationality fit in one bucket. He never said much, but it was his actions that were a witness to his life. However, his acceptance of the Japanese would haunt him for many years.

For most people, Dad was a defender for the underdog. In the 1960's the daughter of our neighbor dated a black man and became pregnant. Not only was there a stigma attached to pregnancy out of wedlock, but it was out of the norm at the time for interracial couples in a predominantly white community. The babies were often not accepted by either the white or the black community—and sometimes neither of them.

Dad was the first one to visit, hold, and spoil those little babies. Their babies were treated like any other infants or children, and their parents and grandparents were accepted. He treated them like he treated everyone else—with respect and dignity.

At his funeral, one such family came and spoke to me. They expressed their love for a man that was there in quiet acceptance, while the rest of the world judged them. Seeing how he treated others made a lasting change in their lives. It served as an example to them of how to treat others they encountered who might be in similar circumstances.

His experiences after the bomb became a turning point which changed his view, as well as the way he lived the rest of his life.

CHAPTER 6

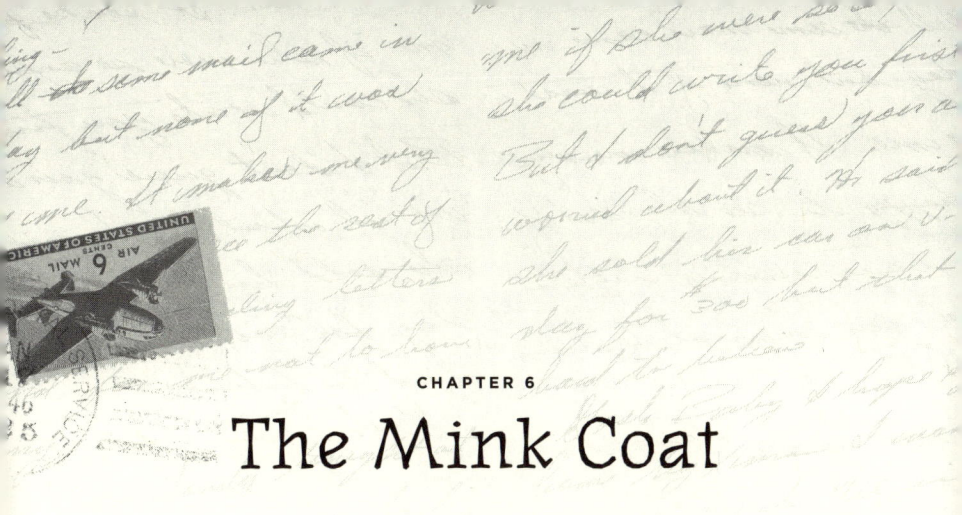

The Mink Coat

I'll buy you that mink coat and new DeSoto.

Aug 11 Labrador

My Darling wife,
Well, I still can't figure it out if Japan surrendered because of the atom bomb or because Russia entered into the war, but I can't help but believe it was because they heard that I was on my way over!

I wish the war being over meant that it was over for me too, but I think we will go on over anyway. It won't be so bad, so I don't want you to worry. We won't have to worry about the Japs but we will have to fight the weather while we are here. The ceiling is really socked in today. We are still weathered in.

You be sure to write and tell me just how everyone reacts to this war being over. I want to hear what they are saying back home.

Sugar it is so hard to write without ever receiving a letter. I'll be so glad when we get into India and I can read my mail from you at least that should bring me a little closer to you. It is hard to go day after day without a letter, not knowing how everyone is.

Nearly all the boys got drunk last night and really tore the place up. There were a few sensible ones and we stayed sober. I think getting drunk is hardly the way to celebrate the victory.

Darling, I've missed you so very much. I'm the luckiest guy in the world to have you to come home to. I'll be so glad when I'm home and have a good job. I'll buy you that mink coat and new DeSoto and I'll be so very proud of you, you'll be my movie star. I guess I have the most beautiful wife in the world. I know I would cry if I weren't sitting in the officer's club.

Say Sugar, you had better sell the car just as quick as you possibly can, we just can't afford to lose all that money we will need it more than ever now.

Love Bill

I find a little humor in these last two paragraphs, although I am sure he didn't mean for it to be funny. He talked about a new mink coat, a new DeSoto, and oh, by the way, he said, "You had better sell the car."

For all their 55 years together, my dad adored my mom. I remember getting miffed at my mom more than once because he was so good to her, and I didn't think she repaid that adoration like I thought she should have. Looking back, I know that she did compensate in the ways that he needed her to.

> I'll buy you that mink coat and new DeSoto.

She was his wife who cleaned his home, ironed his clothes (even his pajamas and his underwear), and had his dinner on the table. She was his companion and the love of his life. She was beautiful and stylish; she was his movie star. She cut his hair, watched his TV shows with him, and was his everything. It was their life, just how they liked it.

Dad would have liked to have had a few more beers or drinks than Mom would allow. She always kept him in check with the liquor. "Buster, you have had two already," she would say. Then he would stop with no argument. Even in these letters, you can see that he wanted to keep their agreement to love, cherish, and obey. He knew it was important to her that he should not get drunk. It was a vow he would keep.

I think he also knew it might make him do things he shouldn't do, and jeopardize what they had. Seeing others get drunk and the way they acted further solidified his belief. Drinking could have been a source of struggle had he not been aware of overdoing it.

My grandfather, Old Dad, did drink, but it wasn't talked about much. He smelled like a combination of cedar wood, fresh mowed grass, and raisins. I always thought that it was Old Spice cologne because that is what I was told. However, it may have been a mix of Old Spice and old whiskey, especially on Saturday nights when I would spend the night.

The family always talked about his wingding's, where he would go to the bars and drink too much. My grandmother would lock him out of the house on those occasions. One night, his daughters went to the location of his wingding and hid his car so he couldn't drive home.

All four of the grown girls and Grandma came into the kitchen laughing, imagining him stumbling around in the dark trying to find his car and having to walk home. The more they talked about it, the more they laughed.

> **Their attitude was "it is what it is."**

I found out later that Old Dad had a lady friend that he would dance and drink with every Saturday night. He never missed a Saturday and would stay out until two in the morning dancing.

Each Sunday morning, he would make up for his Saturday night sins by watching a church service on TV, however, he never graced a physical church building on Sundays. I guess he thought no one on the TV would judge him.

When Old Dad was sick and dying in the hospital, the lady friend came to see him. All the girls kept Grandma busy in the cafeteria so the two would not cross paths.

Grandma was never sad over this, and the girls never held it against their father. Those girls did what they wanted, regardless of what he said. They loved him despite all his flaws, but they were not about to let what he did affect their lives with each other or the family. Their attitude was "it is what it is."

The mink coat for Mom eventually became a reality. I remember when Dad gave it to her. It was a full-length, white mink coat that she proudly modeled. Mom dressed up in her skirt and heels to perform a runway showcase for us in the yard. I don't even think it was the coat she was so fond of at that point; it was the idea that he saved all those years to give it to her.

Since Mom and Dad were not socialites, she did not get to wear that mink coat very often. She would not wear it to the movies because it might get greasy with popcorn; therefore, she only wore it to church on Sundays. I am sure that gave the congregation something to talk about after the service. They saw Dad putting his five dollars in the collection plate and Mom with a new mink coat.

It didn't bother either one of them what other people thought. They didn't care if they were part of the "A" crowd or not. They had their own life, their own family, and their own values that they lived by.

I still have that mink coat. I don't know what to do with it, but I cannot bear to give it away.

Mom and her new mink coat!

CHAPTER 7

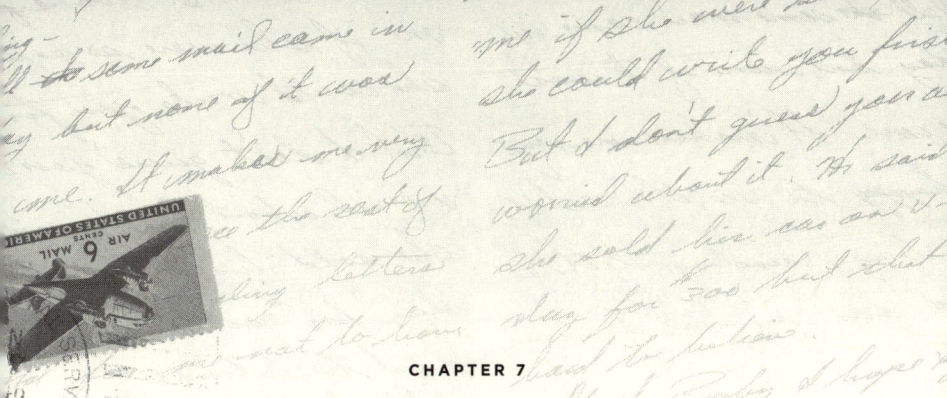

Sondrestrom Air Base, Greenland

Get your butts in here right now!

Monday, Aug 13, 1945

My dearest wife,

Well, Darling we finally got off from Labrador and we are at Greenland now. I thought Labrador was bad but it was paradise compared to this place.

You should see these icebergs! It is as warm here right now as it will ever get and they are still awfully big. Some of them will never melt. It is pretty cold here and no vegetation except a little scrub brush they call tundra.

I'll tell you all I've done today. I got up pretty early and my co-pilot and I went down to the pier and a sergeant took us for a nice boat ride thru the harbor. It was a swell boat; about 70 feet long and had about 4 or 5 bunks and a kitchen underneath. It has a 700 horsepower motor and makes about 30 knots. We sure had to dodge through icebergs. It was a lot of fun. I would like to own one of these when we get home. Let's get one.

They've got Bob Wills on the radio and it sure is corny.

We got some ammunition for our pistols and then we went out and climbed a great mountain. It took us about 3 hours to get to the top. Then we started down and found a nice beautiful spot with a fresh crystal stream running down it and shot up our ammo and came back.

I went to the PX tonight and bought a carton of cigarettes for only 40 cents that was only 4 cents a package.

Ok yes, I almost forgot, I sent out a fountain pen from Bangor Maine.

After I bought it and had mailed it I forgot that your daddy needed one. So you can give it to him? Tell him that will be his birthday present whenever that is.

While in Labrador I saw the new Bogart and Brunel show. "The big sleep" and it was much better than their first one. Be sure to see it when you can. I also saw the movie "A Bell for Adano" but wasn't as good as I thought it would be.

Last night they gave us K rations for supper. So I went fishing because we are right by water and I caught 3 catfish each weighing about 3 pounds and cooked them outside over an open fire for me and the boys. It was pretty good!

I'll bet the people back in the states have really been celebrating the last couple of days. Well, to be honest I haven't been celebrating a bit.

Say baby have you heard "on the sunny side of the street?" It is an old song that has been popular for years. I really like it and know you would too. We can sing it together when I get home.

Oh, Sugar how I miss you. We keep the radio on from 12 noon to 11 at night for that is all there is to do. Every time I hear a song that you use to sing it makes me so sad I want to cry. Darling I think of you every moment and last night I even dreamed of you. I think of how it will be when we first see each other. I have got to close because this kind of talk is breaking my heart.

I must go to sleep now.

Still no letters

Goodnight my Darling, Bill

READING THIS LETTER, I realized that is how Dad made it during these times; how they all made it through the war. They were far from where they wanted to be. His eyes fixed on Mom and family whom he could not see. He had to take his mind and focus away from the temporary to visualize the future that they were going to have.

> We can sing it together when I get home.

It figures that Dad would go fishing and make those K-rations better. Even in tough times, Dad created adventures if things were too quiet.

We learned never to tell our parents we were bored, because we would immediately be sent outside to work. This particular summer my cousins and I were sitting outside deciding what to do so we were not put to work. Dad saw us out there and thought we needed to be riled up a little. He yelled as if we were in trouble, "Get your butts in here right now!" We all were scared out of our boots because we thought we did something wrong and now we were getting caught. I'm sure there was something we had done wrong; we just couldn't figure out what it was.

So with our heads low, tails tucked in, and scared half to death, we filed into the living room one by one, like a chain gang. Dad made us sit quietly in a circle, and he had a chair in the middle of the ring with a roll of toilet paper on it. We could not imagine what in the world was going to happen to us.

We sat there in silent anticipation for a good 30 minutes. Dad was setting the stage that we were in huge trouble. The waiting and waiting for him to talk was agonizing. Finally, he began his lecture in a stern voice, using his deepest baritone to speak. "This house is using far too much toilet paper, and I am of the belief that it is coming from all of you not knowing how to effectively conserve when wiping."

He then began his demonstration of how to conserve by using only one square to wipe. "Tear only one square off at the perforation." Next, he folded the square into a triangle. "This is how you make the point on the end by folding." Then he tore the pointed end of the triangle off. He put his finger into the hole that was made and said, "You wipe like this, with your finger through the hole. Then you use the leftover piece you tore off to clean your finger."

At that point, we all looked at each other and started laughing. He sternly asked, "Why are you all laughing? This is serious." To which we laughed even harder, and so did he.

When we would take family vacations, there would always be a "surprise and delight" moment. He had the flare to make the ordinary into something magical.

As an adult, my two little boys and I went on a road trip with my parents. We were traveling through Bryce Canyon, and we got out to explore a bit. Dad had picked up some arrowheads at a gift shop along the way without telling anyone and stuffed them into his pocket. And when his grandsons weren't looking, he secretly scattered them on the ground.

He told a great, long story about the cowboys and Indians. He explained, "The settlers traveled through this canyon in their covered wagons, and the Indians were watching them on these very cliffs—right where we were standing now. They must have shot their arrows at the cowboys and settlers who were taking their land." Then he pointed out the route they would have probably made, "Why, I bet if you looked hard enough, you might find some of those arrowheads today."

Sure enough, my little guys started looking and guess what they found? Lots of arrowheads! They were excited about each discovery and

Dad's face lit up—those blue eyes shining—every time they picked one up. "Look, look, Old Dad, another one," they would yell. Dad's laughter rang with each find. My boys proudly displayed them in their rooms until they grew up and joined the Marines.

It wasn't until Dad was in the hospital and knew he was dying that he told my boys from where the arrowheads came. David, my oldest son, was in the Marines and home on family leave because we knew Dad was dying. Steve, the youngest, was a teenager and they both had believed all these years that the arrowheads were actually from the Indians traveling through there. Again, Dad chuckled when he confessed. He needed to clear his conscience before he died.

Looking at death could not remove his joy.

> I know a man who is good and kind
> With a splash of hot sauce and the sparkle of wine.
>
> —Ruby Lee

CHAPTER 8

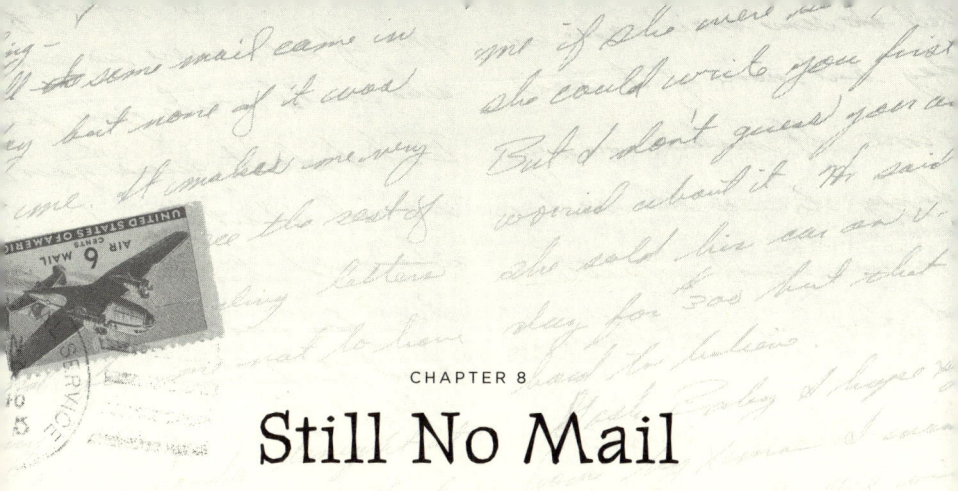

Still No Mail

I nearly froze coming up here.
We were at 8,000 feet and it was 12 degrees.
That is pretty cold for summer isn't it?

August 22, Iceland

Hello Darling

Sorry I couldn't write yesterday but we didn't get up until 10:30 then ate and took off for Iceland. We got here last night and I left my stationery on the plane.

I nearly froze coming up here. We were at 8,000 feet and it was 12 degrees. That is pretty cold for summer isn't it? It isn't so terribly cold here on Iceland though about 55 degrees but there isn't much sun for very long.

There seems to be dampness though and your bed and bedding is damp and it takes a while to get warm when you go to bed. Our blankets feel wet.

We are waiting now for the gas truck then we will take off for Scotland.

Our barracks that we slept in last night looked like bathtubs turned upside down. I'm sure you have seen newsreels of Iceland in the winter where there was so much snow and wind. I remember seeing them.

I've got to go now.

All my love, Bill

The barracks did look like the old-fashioned bathtubs with feet, especially the kind that Dad grew up using in my grandmother's house.

There were five children and one bathroom. It was equipped with a toilet, a pedestal sink, and a bathtub with no shower. The bathtub had rust stains from the water dripping down the inside. When I close my eyes, I can still visualize it today. There was a rubber stopper with a chain attached to it. The other end of the chain was connected to the tub so the stopper would not get lost. To let the water out, you merely pulled up on the chain. The chain and the stopper were my favorite toy when taking a bath there. As soon as the stopper was removed a drain tornado would gurgle down the pipe.

There were two doors to the bathroom, which allowed access from the bedroom on either side. The locks were slide locks that latched from inside the bathroom. There was no magic way to unlock them with a key from the outside. The inhabitant of the bathroom had to be the one to slide the lock to the open position.

> **Grandma didn't want justice; she just wanted quiet.**

Ruby and Dad were always at odds and the bathroom was a place he would choose for tormenting her, knowing that she could not get to him as long as he was locked in the bathroom.

Ruby needed to use that one and only bathroom on several occasions when Dad would decide to lock himself in. He would purposely take his time bathing, shaving, and dressing, while Ruby pounded on the door screaming that Bud (her name for Dad) was hogging the bathroom and not letting her in.

Dad, being the sweet brother, was shaving slowly and mixing his shave cream in the old shaving cream glass with a brush. He would sing at the top of his lungs as he enjoyed his shaving activity, just to further torment, Ruby.

My grandmother never made him stop tormenting Ruby to let her in. In fact, Grandma took the yardstick after Ruby for her beating on the door. Grandma didn't want justice; she just wanted quiet. This furthered Ruby's claim that Dad was Grandma's favorite since he got away with everything.

Ruby only got the justice she sought one time in her life. She retold the story over and over with an enthusiastic giddiness that grew with each new audience.

Dad was a teenager at the time of the incident. Sitting down at the breakfast table one morning he declared, "Biscuits again!" My grandmother did not have a mean bone in her body, but she must have just had enough that day from a surly teen and a husband that had been on a wingding the night before. As Ruby told it, "Grandma's arm just came up and backhanded him without speaking a word."

She loved this story and told it often with great pride and laughter. Her laugh rolled up from her belly to a throaty wail of cheer that Bud got his comeuppance. She felt vindicated for all the times he tortured her. For once, Bud was not the favorite.

> Who took me with her to town one day?
> Who sat me on a stool to play?
> Who put me in the path of harm?
> Then spanked me when I broke my arm?
>   My Mother
> Who cooked by day and sewed by night?
> Who always taught me wrong from right?
> Then took the buttons right off my skirt,
> And sewed them on Bud's new shirt?
>   My Mother
> Who was gentle and kind and ever mild?
> Who spared the rod and spoiled the child?
> Then wielded the yardstick in her wrath,
> Because I wanted to take a bath.
>   My Mother
>   —Ruby Lee

CHAPTER 9

Vinegar on French Fries

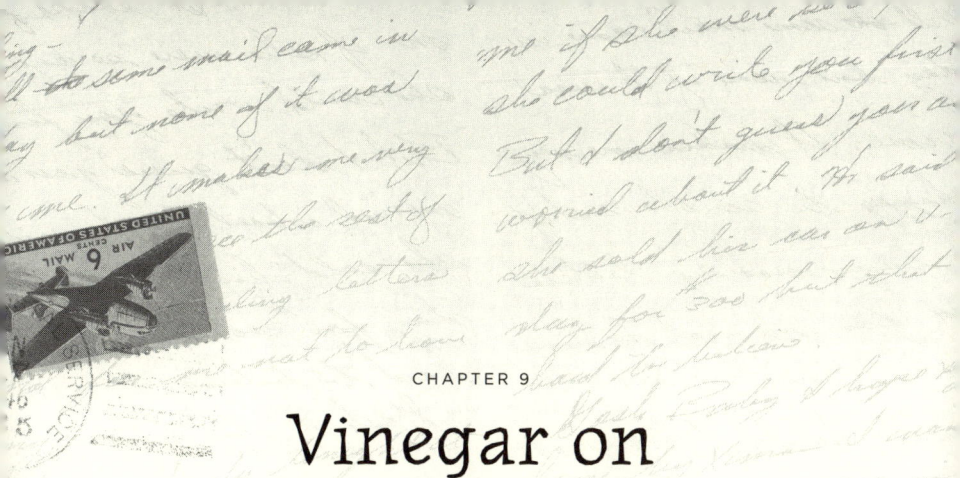

We finally found a small place that only sold French fried potatoes but they called them chips and they started to put vinegar on them. Can you imagine vinegar on French fries?

August 23 Scotland

Hello Darling.
We left Iceland yesterday morning and got here yesterday afternoon. My co-pilot and I cleaned up and went to town. Darling this is beautiful country. It is prettier than any I have ever seen in the states and nearly all the country homes are beautiful. I saw several castles and 2 of them still had moats around them. You know that was when they had water around them to keep out invaders. These homes are beautiful but they would be uncomfortable to live in because they are so old-fashioned.

When we got to town we were terribly disappointed. It looked like the devil. Everything is so dirty and filthy. The dirty kids come up and beg for gum and cigarettes. They were so dirty that their faces and hands were absolutely black. It wasn't only the kids but the town people too. The only places to go here were the skating rink and shows. We went to the ice rink first and I never saw so many ugly female creatures in my life. I was in town from 7 till 12 last night and in all that time I didn't see one decent looking girl.

Don't misunderstand me baby, I wasn't looking for pretty girls but a person can't help but notice.

Then we went to a stage show. All the music they played and sang was ours that they got from the states and every song was at least 10 or 15 years old.

They are terribly old-fashioned in their dress and everything. The people seem awfully ignorant. On the stage the actors would tell some corny joke that would disgust you and these Scots would laugh until their sides would ache. Some actors on the stage would sing a song and the audience would sing right along with them. They would either sing or whistle every time the music started.

Before the show started we tried to get something to eat but there wasn't a café in town that was still open. We finally found a small place that only sold French fried potatoes but they called them chips and they started to put vinegar on them. Can you imagine vinegar on French fries?

I don't know if we will get off today or not. It has started to rain. If we do take off we will go to Marseille France.

Well baby that is about all I know about Scotland.

Oh yes, I wanted to tell you about the toilets we had to use in Iceland. After you had finished going, there was a handle by the commode that you had to pump to mix the dung and the chemicals up. It smelled awful.

Well Sugar, I will see if I can help the boys get the airplane ready. I'm not sure if we will get off today or not.

All my love, Bill

VINEGAR ON FRENCH FRIES had to seem really foreign to a good ol' Oklahoma boy who ate chicken fried steak, homemade biscuits, and chitlin gravy. Hamburgers get served with all the fixings without ketchup or mayo. Mustard is the preferred condiment in Oklahoma.

CHAPTER 9: Vinegar on French Fries

Most of the Cannon's family time revolved around food. There were great gatherings where Grandma would fix homemade donuts. I still have the old donut cutter. It was a round metal biscuit cutter with an insert in it that cut out the hole.

The dough was rolled out and then the donuts were cut and fried. The favorite was the donut holes as they came out of the fryer. Hot from the grease, the holes were rolled in sugar then popped into your mouth. All four sisters would stand around the pan waiting to grab the holes before Dad could. Elbows would be sent to rib cages of the person infringing upon another's territory. Pushing, shoving, and yelling was fair game when it came to getting the hot donuts.

> Dessert was the most important delicacy that life could offer.

The children knew to get out of the way or engage in war time tactics if they were ever to get their fair share of the treats.

While I was growing up, there was always a pie or cake with every meal. Dad knew that dessert was the most important delicacy that life could offer. He raised me with this one fundamental philosophy that he communicated at every meal: "Don't eat so much dinner that you don't have room for dessert." All children got dessert, and no one cared about the sugar rush because we were sent outside to play and burn it off.

The four girls all married, but they continued to gather for meals and dessert at Grandma's house. Grandma bustled around, the girls helped cook, and the men sat in the carport. They sat in rusted metal chairs smoking pipes or cigars waiting for the meal to be ready.

Ruby married a weird duck named Wade. He was quite skinny and never talked much. The one occasion he did decide to speak, ended with Ruby laughing so hard that tears rolled down her cheeks—taking several Kleenex to contain.

There were several delicious chocolate pies served that night, which everyone had devoured; but for one lonely piece leftover. Later that night, Dad went into the kitchen. His heart's desire was on that last piece of pie. As he retrieved it from the cupboard he announced, "Well, there is one lonely piece of pie left. Would anyone else like it?" To that, skinny and quiet Wade answered, "Umm, why yes, I believe I would."

To Ruby, this was almost as good as Dad getting backhanded for the biscuits remark. She yelled at the top of her lungs, "Bud wanted the last piece of pie, but old Wade took it from him!" Wade never did understand why everyone was laughing.

Ruby's marriage to Wade was not a good one. No one ever could figure out why she married him. He was skinny, ugly, and never spoke except for a few words here and there. It was a family mystery to which everyone had an opinion. I heard it speculated that she felt she was getting older, not a real beauty, and wanted a child before time ran out. Wade performed that duty at least once to give her a little boy.

Ruby's "lover" was food. For her, food turned into the enemy to console her in dark hours. She became very heavy, and then food tormented her as much as her relationship with Wade.

> Old Wade is ever patient,
> As courteous as can be.
> But that doesn't ease my
>   own despair;
> I'm desperate to be free.
>   —Ruby Lee

CHAPTER 10

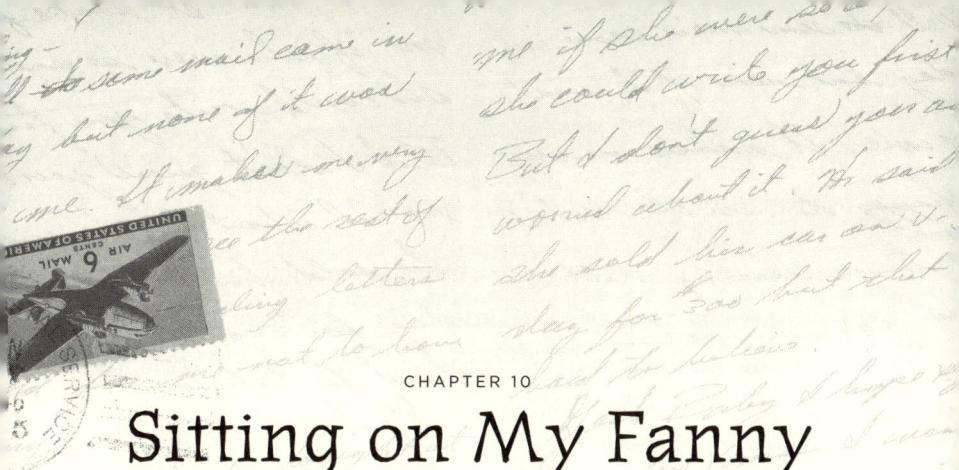

Sitting on My Fanny

*When Mom died she had at least 1,000 scarves
and over 400 pairs of clip- on earrings.
Just deciding what to wear took an hour.*

August 25th Scotland

Dearest Marijo

Well Baby, there isn't much to write. We got our new carburetor and will leave early in the morning. I didn't do much yesterday. Art and I went into Prestwick and saw a British show last night. It was awfully cheaply made and the actors weren't very good.

These guys have been coming in around 5 to 7 every morning and telling some pretty wild tales about these Scottish girls. From what they say they are pretty easy to make. Jones (my radio operator) is arguing with Smith trying to get him to go tonight. Jones likes these girls and doesn't want to go by himself.

They use different words for things over here. One boy said he was on the train sitting next to a girl and she asked him what he had been doing and he told her he had been sitting around on his fanny. Well the girl's face turned red and she didn't say another thing to him. He finally found out that it meant the other side of the body and on a female only.

We take off for France tomorrow. I sure wish we would sit still long enough to get mail.

All my love, Bill

When Dad took his oath to love, honor, and cherish, he also listened to the part that said "forsaking all others."

No one would have ever known if he wandered off with one of those Scottish women except Dad himself. He would have known, and that would have changed him. He did enjoy hearing about the "wild tales" of the other men though.

Dad's sisters all loved Mary Jo (the proper spelling). They brought her into their fold as a sister—not a sister-in-law. She was totally opposite from them and they loved her in spite of that.

Mom was fancy. With that fanciness came hours of preparation to stay that way. It took her hours to be ready for the day. Every day she needed to complete the hair, makeup, proper dress, jewelry that matched every outfit, and a scarf to top it off. Dad loved that about her. He waited patiently for his queen to arrive from her boudoir perfectly attired for his eyes only. That was his vow to cherish. When Mom died she had at least 1,000 scarves and over 400 pairs of clip-on earrings. Just deciding what to wear took an hour. By contrast, Dad's sisters took 10 minutes to be ready and out the door.

Mom didn't like to play or watch sports; she didn't like to get dirty, or messed up in any way. The sisters pretty much engaged in anything the men did and were determined to be better at it than the men were as well.

Mom married into a wild family, which meant that she had to learn to duck and hide to keep from getting into the mix of chaos. The Cannon family reunions usually ended with someone in the pool with or without their clothes on. One such reunion had Mom locking herself in the bathroom because the Cannon's got into a wild brawl. The men were throwing each other into the pool, clothes and all. The women decided it looked like fun and disrobed down to their bras and girdles to join in.

Mom did not want to get her hair wet, not to mention that her makeup would be ruined, nor did she approve of disrobing in front of anyone. Mom ended up in her self proclaimed prison for several hours until she felt safe to come out.

Men of this era were respectful to women therefore being a Southern gentleman also meant that you never called the private body parts by their correct names. I guess the Scottish had that same tradition, and these poor soldiers had no clue that they were saying anything wrong. It makes me giggle to think about the boy on the train trying to make small talk with a foreign girl. She must have thought he was a pervert talking about her private parts.

In the South, the word tallywacker is slang for a man's penis as is the word "jimmy". Tallywacker is in the Urban Dictionary, however, jimmy is not.

On one occasion a family brought over their little baby to our house who's name was Jimmy. There was always a giggle from the family when "Jimmy" arrived. My mom's brother, being a small little guy at the time said, "That's not a Jimmy, that's a baby." I guess he thought everyone was crazy calling a baby by that name.

Mom's baby brother was born when she was 19 years old. He was an "oopsie" baby. Her mom was 42 when she got pregnant. Mom told me she was so embarrassed that her mother was going to have a baby. She could not bear to think of her mom and dad doing the nasty.

After the baby was born, they named him Terry. Mom's parents couldn't have loved any baby more. He was the refreshing joy in all of their lives.

Mom's mother died when Terry was 17. Her death made Mom even more of a mother figure in Terry's life. She adored him and he loved her. Their mother's name was Tiny, and that was her real name. I did not get to know this grandmother very well because I was only eight when she died.

Tiny, as far as they could tell passed out while drawing a bath and fell into the tub. Tiny had a brain tumor and was preparing to go to the Mayo Clinic. Mom had been trying to call her because she was on her way over to take her to the doctor because they suspected she had a brain tumor

Mom had to break into the house and found her mom dead in the bathtub. It wasn't something she talked about much, but it had to be an awful memory to live with. Looking back, I think Mom was tougher than I ever gave her credit for.

> Mary has a mindset
> Against change, I have heard
> She hasn't changed as yet
> She is one old-fashioned bird
>
> Only Lipton tea is good
> Everything ironed a must
> Fixing her hair for the neighborhood
> Before the beauty shop entrust
>
> Mary and I have had lots of laughs
> And memories to treasure
> Cleaning and ironing are her crafts,
> with what she has to measure.
> —Ruby Lee

CHAPTER 11

War Can Make Everyone Act Ugly

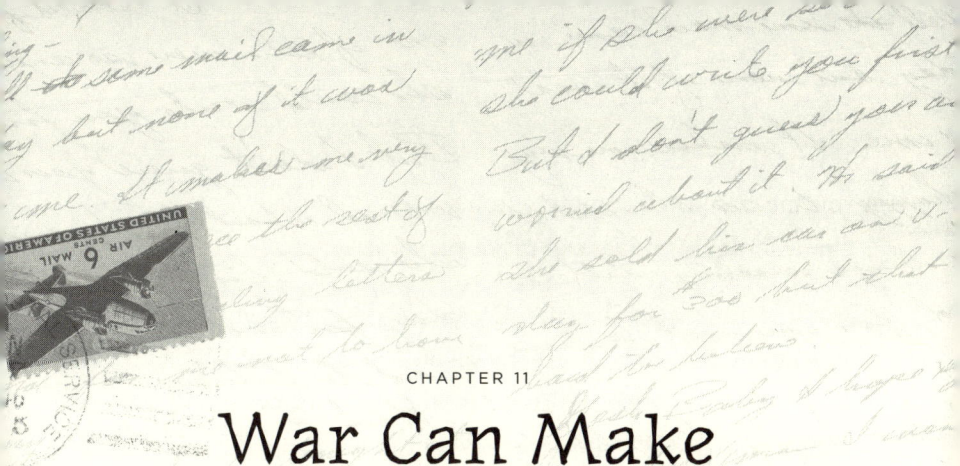

*More than that though was the fact that
Gaines was Dad's friend, and Dad was his friend.*

Sunday, Aug 26th

Hello Darling,

I am now in France. I'm not going into Marseille because I'm too tired.

They say that Marseille has a population of 500,000 and 400,000 of them are whores and that 53% of the V.D. in all the European theater is contracted between here and Paris.

This is a filthy place. All the French people I have seen except the girls working at the PX and mess hall look and smell as though they haven't had a bath in a year or longer.

We went down to the motor pool and got a truck and driver and he took us out to the beach and then into a small town about 3 miles from the base.

These American Negroes stationed here are in heaven. We saw several of them with French girls. They really like that stuff. I hope they like it so well that they just stay over here.

Well Baby, I'm going to take a bath now. We take off for Tripoli at 7 in the morning.

Love you Baby,

Your pretty boy Bill

DAD RAISED ME NOT TO hate, fear, or talk bad about any race. So this mean-spirited comment in his letter I thought was way out of character for him. War can make everyone act ugly.

Where I grew up in Shawnee, Oklahoma, there was white and black separation. In Oklahoma, there was still racial bias, and most talked poorly about black people. They used the ugly slang word for the black people who lived on the other side of the railroad tracks outside of town. But Dad never hesitated to drive to black town, and we did it often to visit his friend Gaines.

My entire family, including my grandmother, knew Gaines and would give what we could to help him. My grandmother would state proudly that she even hugged Gaines and his family, something an Okie at that time would never do.

Gaines had a wife and two little girls. He worked as a mechanic in my grandfather's garage. Just before Christmas every year, we would sit in my room as a family to go through my toys and clothes to give up what I could do without having. I wasn't just required to choose things I didn't want anymore. I was to give more before I could get more. I was also to think of Gaines' children and picture in my mind what toys they would enjoy.

During the summer, my grandmother had a huge garden. It was more than an acre, and she grew vast amounts of food. At harvest she would gather enough fresh produce to take to Gaines and his family. She would can enough tomatoes and vegetables for all of us, the pantry, and for Gaines.

> **I was taught to judge people by their actions and not by the way they looked.**

The relationship was more than just helping a family out, it was the fact that Gaines was Dad's friend, and Dad was his friend. They cared about each other. Dad taught me that Gaines was our family, no matter his color.

I was taught to judge people by their actions and not by the way they looked. My parents were often put to the test to practice what they preached. That didn't mean that they wouldn't say something about the way people looked, and right to their face. A cousin of mine was one of those "long-haired" hippies in the '70s. He lived with Mom and Dad for a short while. They had plenty to say, but they never told him to cut his hair. They just had him sneak out of the house after dark so the neighbors wouldn't see him.

Piercings were another issue. Dad would say to another of my cousins with a pierced lip, "Good gosh, why do you have to have that thing stuck in your lip like that? Don't you have enough common sense to know that it looks like hell?" But he never told him to get rid of it.

This little outburst caused my other cousins to get fake lip rings. They all wore them to the next family dinner.

The lesson for me was not to dislike anyone based merely on his or her looks, and not to take life so seriously.

CHAPTER 12

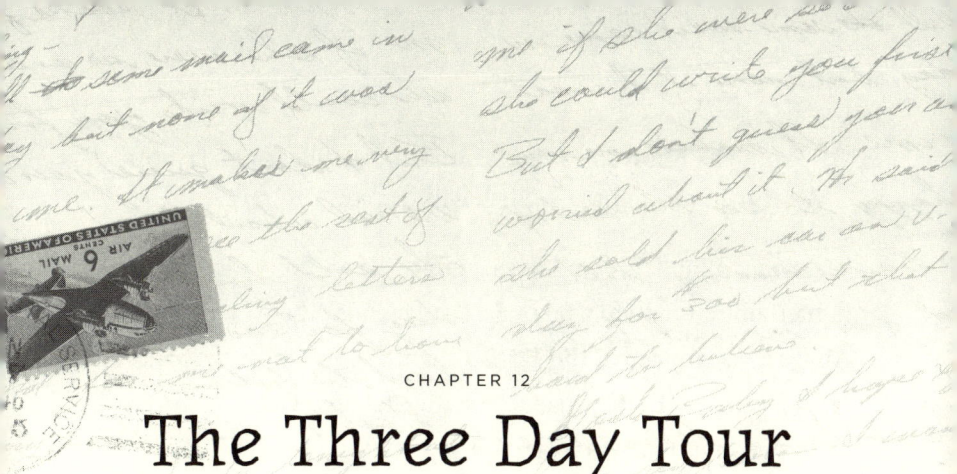

The Three Day Tour

*Some of them have camels and
some of them have a donkey that is no bigger
than a Great Dane dog.*

Tripoli, Libya
August 28th, 1945

Dearest Maryjo

Well, yesterday we landed on "the shores of Tripoli." I'm sending you a piece of paper about the history of this place. After you read it, send it to mother. She will enjoy reading it.

This is quite a place! We went to town and on the way we saw the Arabs who live in small huts and wear what looks like sheets made out of burlap, like two gunny sacks. They are awfully filthy. Some of them have camels and some of them have a donkey that is no bigger than a Great Dane dog.

All of the buildings are made out of mud. They are like stucco at home. The Muslims built some awfully nice buildings in town here. They are very pretty but they weren't built to last. The harbor here is full of sunken German and Italian ships and a lot of the buildings here have big shell holes in them.

The barracks are pretty nice. I wish I had a camera. The Mediterranean Ocean is beautiful; it is sort of a metallic blue.

I am lonely. We are taking off for Cairo soon. I wish I had a letter and some mail from home.

Love Bill

From the Shores of Montezuma to the Shores of Tripoli
We fight our country's battles in the air, on land, and sea.

Welcome to Mullah, Tripolitania, Libya. This airport was one time a fighter aircraft base for Italy's Fascist Legions. The American Ninth Air Force Army aided the British Eighth Army in conquering this territory from the Germans and the Italians. General Rommel's main headquarters was in Tripoli.

In 1815, the United States Marines came to "the shores of Tripoli" and obtained a treaty with the Barbary Pirates which assure the safety of American sailing ships.

The city was founded about 700 BC by the Phoenicians. Wow, a long time ago!

There was also a Roman period from 140 BC to 450 AD. Julius Caesar conquered all of present day Libya and there was a long period of peace.

August 29th

My Darling Marijo

Cairo is some place I guess. It is the most fascinating city I have ever been in. It has many modern buildings. They are all stucco of course because they have no wood.

When we got to town we got off the bus at the Sheppard Hotel. The Sheppard is quite famous because all the officers stay there. We got out in front of the hotel and no less than 8 or 10 Arabs gathered around us and tried to sell us souvenirs. They bother you to death and if you don't go into the hotel they will follow you all over town. They like us pilots!

The kids come up and throw mud on your shoes and tell you that you need a shoe shine and if you don't buy it they will throw mud on your clothes.

CHAPTER 12: The Three Day Tour

We hired a guide and a taxi and went out to the pyramids and sphinx. That is really something. The pyramids are 451 feet high and I don't know how big around. The sphinx is a head of a woman, the face of a man, and the body of a lion. It was really a sight.

We are leaving now.

All my love, Bill

August 30th

Dearest Mary jo

We made it here to Abadan Iran. We will leave soon for Karachi. It is a pretty long hop, about 1200 or 1300 miles.

It is really hot here. It was about 125 in the shade. There is no telling how hot it was in the sun because a thermometer would break in the open.

We were fortunate enough to get an air conditioned barracks though and it was really nice inside. This is supposed to be the hottest place in the world.

When we get our assignments, we will have a new address. I'll send it to you as soon as possible.

We have met some ATC pilots who came from Karachi and they all said there were more pilots than they knew what to do with.

Say sugar, how did our picture come out? I had nearly forgotten about it. I do hope they were good.

Well sugar I'll stop now and try to get this mailed from here. Still no mail. I am getting P.Oed.

Bill

THIS WAS ONLY A 3-DAY TRIP and Dad got to see so many things in that short amount of time.

The Cairo airbase shared the infrastructure with the Sphinx, which gave him easy access for sightseeing.

In the short period of two weeks, he was in Iceland, the coldest place, and then to Abadan, the hottest place.

He was not worried about the events of the world. He was a young country boy, impetuous, and way outside his field of knowledge. He was a hotshot pilot seeing the world.

Dad was a big fish in the small pond at Shawnee High School. He was known as "Buck" the star tackle-guard. He was praised for his good looks, wavy hair, in addition to being a nice guy. A cocky but funny ego went along with "Buck." Now he was equipped with Silver Wings that made him feel like an even bigger fish in an even a bigger pond.

Because of his "status" in high school, he could clear out the classroom by insisting his teachers do things his way, or else his entire football squad would leave class with him. He told his teacher with a big smile on his face, "Alva, if Mary Jo doesn't read some more poetry then we are leaving right now. Us boys like poetry to give us some class."

He was a big fish in a small pond.

CHAPTER 12: **The Three Day Tour** 69

Dad and his football team.

Mom had to stand up in class to deliver a poetry reading or the entire football team would once again leave class.

He was mischievous and fun, naughty but likable, with a big smile that accompanied a big ego.

Hometown boy get's Silver Wings

Gets Silver Wings

A-C William R. Cannon, son of Mr. and Mrs. W. O. Cannon of Richmond, Calif., formerly of Shawnee, was graduated recently as a pilot and flight officer from Blackland army air field, Waco, Tex., and is spending a 16-day furlough with his wife at 623 North Park.

Cannon, who will report December 6 at Frederick, Okla., has been in service 18 months. He was graduated from Shawnee high school in 1942 where he was a football star and was a News-Star carrier boy.

His father, W. O. Cannon, is in the coast guard at Richmond, Calif. His wife is the former Miss Mary Jo Cook.

70 Buster the Football Flyboy

Dad's flight training logs.

CHAPTER 12: The Three Day Tour

INDIVIDUAL FLIGHT RECORD

(1) SERIAL NO. T-123370 (2) NAME CANNON WILLIAM RAYMOND (3) RANK Flt/O (4) AGE 1912
(5) PERS. CLASS 17 (6) BRANCH AIR CORPS (7) STATION Bowman FLD AT
(8) ORGANIZATION ASSIGNED AAF ITCC GLIDER CRA TRAINING CENTER
(9) ORGANIZATION ATTACHED
(10) PRESENT RATING & DATE GLIDER PILOT 11/26/43 (11) ORIGINAL RATING & DATE GP 11/26/43
(12) TRANSFERRED FROM (13) FLIGHT RESTRICTIONS
(15) TRANSFERRED TO (14) TRANSFER DATE

(17) MONTH DEC 1943

DAY	AIRCRAFT TYPE, MODEL & SERIES				CO-PILOT		FIRST PILOT DAY	NIGHT	RATED PERS. NON-PILOT						NIGHT		
3	CG-4A	5			2:15					:30					2:15		
4	CG-4A	2			:55										:55		
11	CG-4A	2			1:20												
14	CG-4A	1			1:05										1:05		

CERTIFIED CORRECT:
J. R. GOODLOE
Flt/O., Air Corps
Ass't Operations Officer

COLUMN TOTALS 5:35 4:15
(42) TOTAL STUDENT PILOT TIME (43) TOTAL FIRST PILOT TIME (44) TOTAL PILOT TIME
(37) THIS MONTH 5:35
(38) PREVIOUS MONTHS THIS F.Y. 0:00 44:45
(39) THIS FISCAL YEAR 44:45 50:20
(40) PREVIOUS FISCAL YEARS 112:35 0:00 112:35
(41) TO DATE 157:20 162:55

Dad in the flight school flying air trainer.

CHAPTER 6: The Mink Coat   73

*Army Air Forces
Advanced Pilot School
at
Pecos Army Air Field
Pecos, Texas
announces the graduation of
Class 44-D
Saturday morning, April fifteenth
Nineteen hundred and forty-four
at ten o'clock
South Hangar*

United States Army Air Forces

Graduation announcement from class of 44-D. Right: Dad's graduation picture from the Air Force Academy.

Mom and Dad just married while he was in flight school.

CHAPTER 13

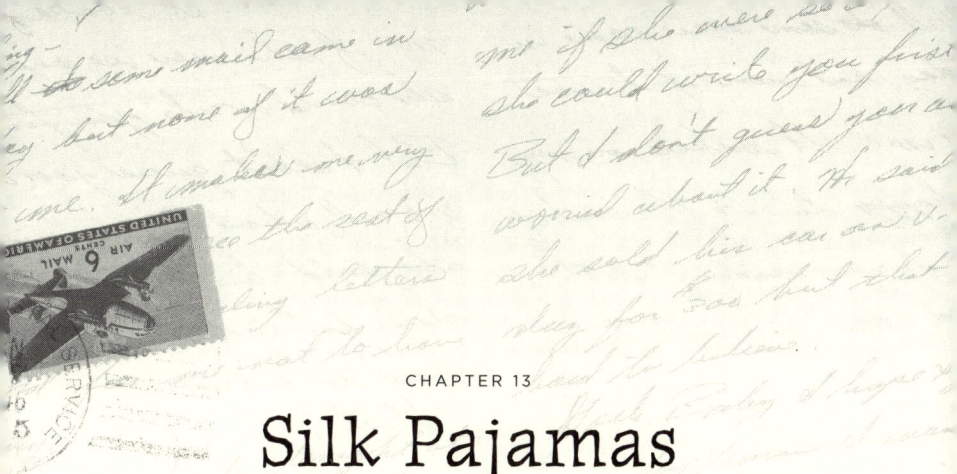

Silk Pajamas

*Buster, look what you are teaching these kids—
that it is OK to lie.*

Sept 2, 1945

Dearest Maryjo

Wel,1 darling, we arrived at Karachi and all I have to say is this is one hell of a place!

The biggest disappointment is that we don't have any mail here. I thought surely we would get it here but it is being sent on to our permanent station. Just where that is, I don't know but it will be several days before they send us on.

The toilets are outside and the smell of them is horrible. The food isn't so terribly bad though. What goes in must come out though.

We went to town last night and had some very good steaks at the officers club in town.

We saw some of these Indian women yesterday and a lot of them had rings in their noses. They look a lot like Negroes except usually don't have the thick lips and flat noses.

I bought some Karachi boots yesterday. They are really nice. They are about like my flying boots only a little higher. I've been trying to get you something but all their bed jackets, pajamas and such look very pretty from a distance but when you look at them close, the embroidery work looks cheap. I know you wouldn't like anything I have seen yet. I started to get you an opal ring last night but it had a big chip out of it.

They say in China you can really get some beautiful silk things. So I think I will just wait and maybe I'll get something there. The things are very expensive from 15 to 35 dollars for P.J's and I am sure for that price you could find something at home you like better.

All my love, Bill

AT THE END OF MY MOM'S LIFE, I acted like a brat again because I still was holding onto bitterness about her attitude of what I interpreted as selfishness. Mom wanted my time, that is all. I felt she was being selfish and spoiled. Didn't she know how over burdened I was taking care of business and children?

What I now realize is that my dad lifted her up to that position for 55 years. She loved the beautiful bed jackets; he loved them on her. He enjoyed seeing her dressed in the finest for him. He wanted the embroidery to be worthy of her. He didn't want her to own a chipped ring. He wanted her to have what she wanted. So after 55 years of this, why would I think that she would not want what he had wanted for her all these years?

The Karachi boots were a big deal to Dad. He even mentioned them later in his life, stating that they were very sharp and looked like what the Brits wore. He was especially animated when he told me they were not regulation boots, but the flyboys didn't always obey regulation rules. Dad liked to break the rules slightly and cheat on games just for fun to see if you would catch him.

> Devoted husband and loving father
> I may be biased for he's my brother
> The jackpot he hit so early in life
> Was his incredible luck in choosing
>   a wife.
>
> —Ruby Lee

CHAPTER 13: Silk Pajamas

Even when I was young, I learned to watch him like a hawk when we played Monopoly. It only took a few times letting Dad be the banker to discover why he never ran out of money.

Dad also didn't care that my cousins and I lost the game. My cousins and I would whine and cry and yell at him, calling him a cheater. He would laugh and rake in the money with his hands chanting, "I won, I won," in his loud voice.

It wasn't uncommon for our growing family to vacation together. He thought nothing about piling my cousins into the car as we headed out for our next "adventure." One time, he slipped a piece of petrified wood from the Petrified Forest into his pocket while we were on vacation—something that we kids had learned from the ranger was a definite "no-no" to do. He secretly pocketed a silver dollar sized piece while no one was looking.

As we exited the park, the park ranger stopped all the cars as they left. Seeing kids in the station wagon and asked, "No one took any objects out of the park now did they?" We all looked half scared to death and nodded our heads no. "No, sir." Dad answered, "I watched these kids the whole time."

> No one took any objects out of the park now did they?

As soon as we got away from the ranger station, Dad pulled out the petrified wood and laughed about what he found in his pocket. Mom scorned, "Buster, look what you are teaching these kids—that it is OK to lie."

"I didn't lie," he laughed, "the kids didn't take anything from there."

I still have the petrified wood.

I never thought Dad had an ego, but all of my boyfriends and later my husband would say he had a huge one. In fact, he pretty much scared the pee-waddling out of them at first. Not because he was mean, but because he was a bigger-than-life kind of guy commanding the air around him. He never needed to yell at us kids; he would just let us know we had been caught. Then he would let us simmer in our own juice for a bit.

One summer night we were out as a group just hanging out, driving around, and having fun. We didn't want to come in at 10 p.m., which was my curfew. I phoned Dad to say we had had a flat tire but we were changing it, so we'd be about an hour late. This just proves that the frontal cortex isn't formed yet in teenagers .... no matter how smart they are.

> What kind of new hand cleaner did you all find to get all the black off your hands so well?

Upon arriving home, Dad was waiting for us on the porch. He was smiling and said so sweetly, "Hey, come on inside a minute."

We entered the den and sat in silence on the couch. We were looking at each other as Dad made small talk. Finally, he asked, "What kind of new hand cleaner did you all find to get all the black from the tire off of your hands so well? I know I could get the dealerships to buy some good cleaner like that!"

I was the one who confessed that we just wanted to stay out a little later. I knew not to make excuses, but I also knew that I would not have to worry about a curfew for a week or so because I wouldn't be going out.

We moved to Denver when I was 13 because Dad took a job with Chrysler Corporation as the zone manager, which made him pretty high ranking with the car dealerships.

As a single adult I needed a car, so having him assist with the dealership buying process was a given. We drove into the lot and Dad pulled right into the owner's parking space. From the window of the dealership, my future husband was watching the scenes unfold thinking, "Who is this guy with the nerve to park in the owner's parking spot?"

I pointed out the vehicles that I liked and Dad went into the dealership, sat on the corner of the general manager's desk, then proceeded to dictate the terms of the sale. By now my future husband was totally intimidated, and quite afraid to ask me out now. It took some time for him to get up the nerve to talk to me.

Buster was continuing his command in life from a high school football star to a successful flyboy, and now a high ranking zone manager. Even in the face of death, he respectfully commanded God to hurry, which God did.

CHAPTER 14

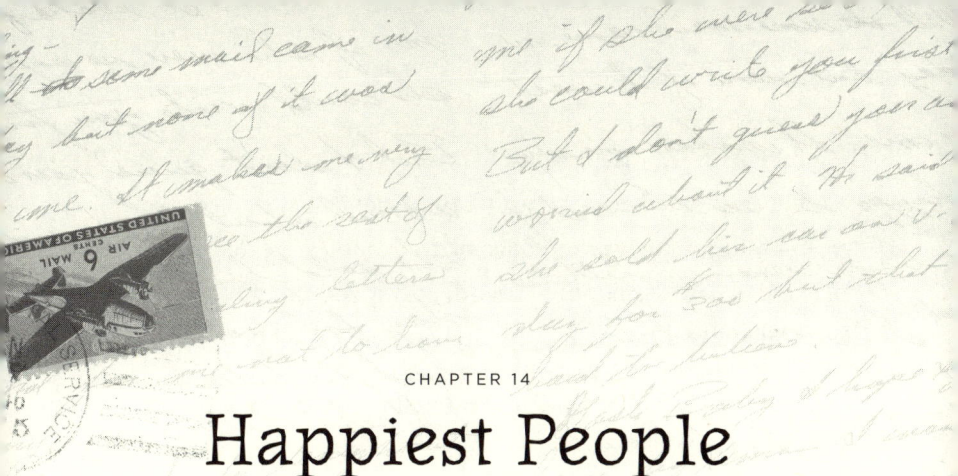

Happiest People

I wanted her to tell him,
it was OK to go, but she couldn't.

Monday, Sept 3rd, 1945 Karachi

Hello Darling

Oh baby, how I have missed you. It seems more like a year since I left you at Bergstrom. I don't know how much longer I can go like this, without mail. I don't' know what you are doing or anything. The old saying that "absence makes the heart grow fonder" is true.

I love you more than I can put into words. At night I lie in bed and think of the affectionate things I will write you, but then when I sit down to write, this old pen won't write what I think and what I can feel.

Darling, we are so very lucky and fortunate to have had each other for those few glorious months. When I think of those so called practical couples that waited until the war is over, I feel sorry for them. Of course being overseas may be a little harder on me than on them but I at least have my memories and best of all I have my plans for us when I get home.

Baby, we will be the happiest two people in the world. You and I are inseparable.

Love you more than ever, Buster

My parents were inseparable. As his life was coming to an end, it was not easy for either of them. Of course, none of us wanted to let him go, but for Mom, it was letting go of everything she ever had. He was all she had. He was her only friend, only love, and only job. He was what filled her days, nights, and in between for her entire life.

I wanted Mom to tell Dad it was OK to go, but she couldn't. She was making it harder for him to let go. She climbed into his hospital bed, holding him, crying on his chest. Tears soaked his freshly ironed pajamas. We could not pry her away and Dad was holding on even though he wanted to leave because he didn't like to fight against what she wanted.

There was only one serious fight that I can remember between my mom and dad. They had arguments from time to time, but this particular battle over biscuits was the only time I ever remember my mom crying and my dad storming out of the house. I also remember standing up for my dad because Mom was being so mean.

Mom never worked outside the home in their marriage except for a short stint early on as a phone operator. She also worked a bit to pay back money they borrowed money from Dad's sister Syd for the move to Denver. Mom needed to work to help pay back that loan.

Mom wasn't good at working outside of the home. I mean she did an excellent job when she did work, but working was not her cup of tea. It took her two hours just to get dressed for work because she had to look perfect, so add that to an eight hour day and you have one tired and cranky wife.

> **He was being sweet to make dinner, and she was being ugly and unappreciative.**

She got home later than Dad, so he would make dinner. One night he had made biscuits and he had not done it right, so my mom got into a fight with him over the way he made the biscuits.

That didn't sit well with Dad. He became so irritated that she would get mad over the biscuits that he stormed out of the house, which he had never done before. Then I got into the fight with Mom because she was being ugly to my dad! He was being sweet to make dinner, and she was being ugly and unappreciative.

Looking back, I realized that they probably both had had a long and tiring day, and the biscuits were the straw that broke the camel's back. I guess the reason this story came to mind was that last sentence Dad wrote in his letter of September 3, 1945: "Baby, we will be the happiest two people in the world." And they really were—except for the biscuits incident.

Happiest people, Mom and Dad.

Happiest People

There is a word that I hear often
A word that has the power to soften
The saddest days are always brightened
The most despondent times are lightened

This word makes true the golden years
And always dries those bitter tears
It validates my life as I grow old
It keeps me young so I've been told

Love —Grandma Cannon

CHAPTER 15

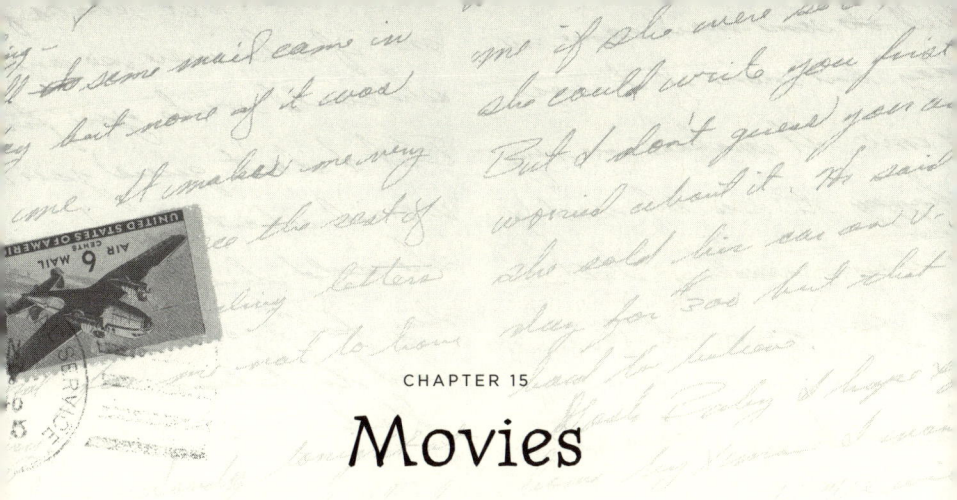

Movies

*That was a good one!
It is the kind you would like because
it is deep and mysterious.*

Wed Sept 8th, 1945 Karachi

Dearest Maryjo

Hello sugar, I have been assigned a detail for a while, while I am here. They have made me a finance officer for a week. There isn't much to do. About the only thing I have to do is witness and sign when an enlisted man gets a partial payment. There is a lot of that because this is a transit center for both the personnel going home and coming in. It is very boring and makes the day go by so slow.

I would be enjoying my life of relaxation here if only they would send us our mail, but they say that it is impossible. I just don't understand why we cannot get our mail. You don't know how hard it is to go so long without word from you or anyone.

The other night I saw "Suspect" with Charles Laughton and Ella Raines. I think that is the one you saw and liked so well in Austin while I was on a cross country. I thought it was a very good picture.

Last night I saw "the story of Dorian Grey." That was a good one! It is the kind you would like because it is deep and mysterious.

I think they are showing "It's a Pleasure" with that skating star tonight.

I haven't been to town again since the first time and I don't plan to go. It is too much trouble to take the bother to clean up and catch a bus, especially after you've been there once.

Some of the boys don't think we will be over here for a year even. They think that we will go home after about a month but I don't know. Victory meant for us that our ships just wouldn't be shot at which is quite a bit and should keep you from worrying.

I just was alerted that we may have to leave. We are going to the 1st combat cargo in Burma. I am a little disappointed because I wanted to go to China. But at least I will be getting out of here and maybe get some mail.

Love you more than ever, Bill

MOVIES! This letter just made me realize why films were so important to Dad and Mom. They connected through the movies they watched, whether together or apart. My parents loved movies! Every Saturday afternoon they would go to the movies until he died.

Mom would tell me about the old days saying, "Movies were a dime for a double feature. We would go to a matinee and have nickel popcorn and coke. Even when we had our babies with us, we could go upstairs to the balcony that had glass where we could enjoy the show."

> **He must have learned the hiding trick from Old Dad.**

Their Saturday routine was always the same. Dad got up early and played golf with his friends. Then he'd have a few beers on the golf course that he would not tell Mom about. He'd also have a forbidden pack of cigarettes tucked into his golf bag.

He must have learned the hiding trick from Old Dad. As kids, we would go out to the barn and find Old Dad's whiskey bottle he hid there so he could sneak himself a swig now and again. We loved to find it and re-hide it somewhere else so he couldn't locate it.

CHAPTER 15: Movies

Dad also learned to hide things as a small child when he would visit his granny, who was never without snuff in her lip. One day he decided to steal Granny's snuff; then hid behind the barn to have himself a dip. He got no sympathy when he got sick either. It served him right for stealing Granny's snuff.

Mom knew the cigarettes were going to kill him. She was constantly on him about smoking, and he was constantly hiding them from her. She would find them in his socks, toolbox, old flower pots, and pretty much any place he thought she wouldn't look.

Dad would put his cigarette ashes in the cuffs of his pants if he was sneaking around and was afraid he'd get caught. Then he would forget to empty the cuffs, and Mom would once again bust him for smoking.

When you could still smoke indoors, he would smoke at his job. I went to visit him at work and he quickly shut his desk drawer as I walked in. Smoke was billowing out of his drawer and he kept talking to me like nothing at all was going on. He had that shit-eating grin on his face and he asked, "What are you up to?"

I had a hard time not laughing and pointed to his drawer. "Dad, what are you up to is the question?"

He just answered by talking about his job. "I'm calling customers to see how their service was, and chatting with the nicest folks." All the while, smoke was still funneling out of the drawer.

Smoke continued until I had to leave. I walked around the desk to give him a hug and a kiss to discover he reeked reeked of smoke and Trident gum.

After his golf game, he would do lawn work and then clean up for their Saturday night date—a movie with popcorn and a Coke. It was the highlight of their week, and the movie was always discussed afterward. They talked about the star, the plot, and the message behind the movie.

He would always bring home leftover popcorn to have for breakfast the next morning. He filled up a big glass with popcorn, added sugar, and topped it off with whole milk. Managing to do this before Mom was awake was vital because a secret cigarette at the end made the feast complete.

Even after Dad died we would take Mom to the movies every Saturday. Sometimes it was the only time she would get out and have the company of another person. I can remember most of the times I would not want to take her to the movies because we wanted to go somewhere else on Saturday, but I felt an obligation to get her out of the house to do something she would enjoy. Shame on me! I just didn't realize what movies meant to her … and to them. How dare I be so selfish not wanting to go!

Movies had been a part of their lives from the start in her family. Mom and her sister would create scrapbooks of all the movie stars by gathering used movie posters from the theater. They didn't have money for real scrapbooks, so she would get old parts catalogs from their daddy's dealership that were being thrown out to paste the pictures onto them.

Movies were not action films or computer graphics; they were stories to escape in. They depicted the feelings of the era. They made you think and feel—laugh and cry. I wish I had realized this sooner.

Chilton-old parts book used as scrapbook.

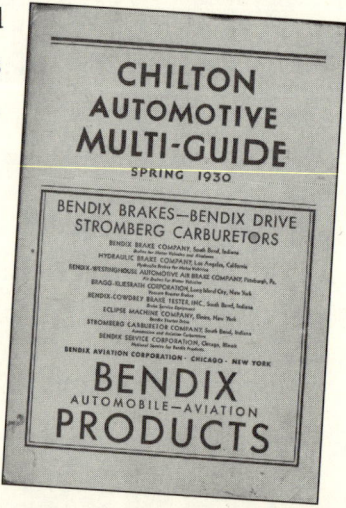

CHAPTER 15: Movies 89

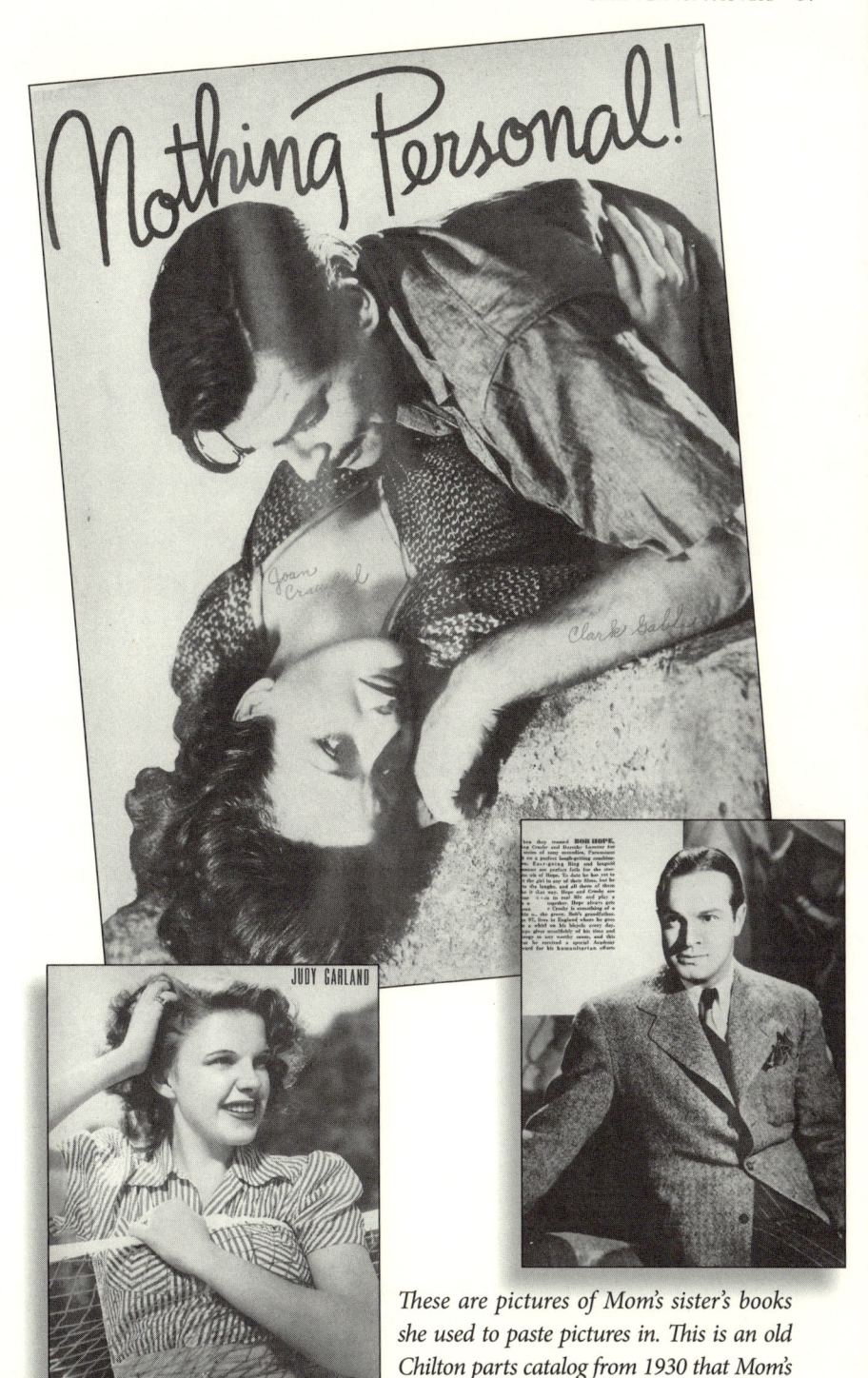

These are pictures of Mom's sister's books she used to paste pictures in. This is an old Chilton parts catalog from 1930 that Mom's father had at the dealership he worked.

CHAPTER 16

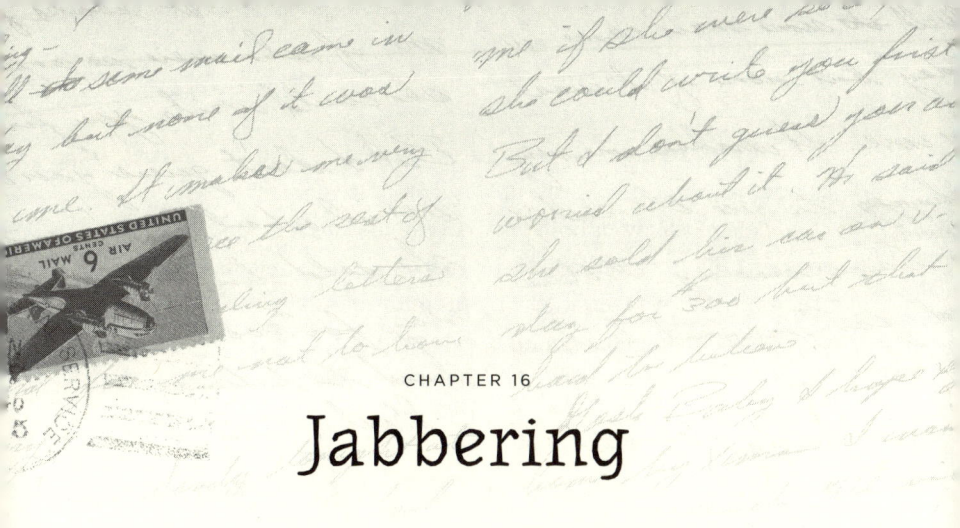

Jabbering

... they jabber all the time. I sure do get sick of it.

Sept 13th

My Darling Wife

Sugar I'm so darn disgusted I don't know what to do. We went to Burma where we were assigned and found out the group we were assigned to have moved out to China. I don't know when we will get to wherever we're supposed to go.

We finally found out for sure where the 1st Combat Cargo Group is. It is in Liuzhou. That is who we are supposed to be assigned to. We will move mostly food and supplies. We are alerted and may leave from there this afternoon.

The boys from there say we will sleep in tents and will have a dirt floor. I don't care where we sleep; I will just be glad to get up there and start to work. This being unsettled is getting the best of me. When we get there I will get a permanent address and then I'll be able to get some mail. I'm pretty sure the address I'll use on this letter will be right except for the squadron.

This Squadron is rumored to move to Shanghai in about a month. I certainly hope so. It would be much nicer there.

Last night I saw "Weekend at the Waldorf". It was a good show.

Darling I have a lot of work to do. We have to string up lights and everything. So I had better get busy. Write and tell me everything and be sure to send me the mail returned to you.

> There are a bunch of Chinese officers next to us and they jabber all the time. I sure do get sick of it.
>
> I also lost my billfold with all my pictures, money, and everything in it. But the thing that P.O.'s me the most is the thought that we won't get any mail for a long time.
>
> Now darling if that mail is returned to you be sure to send me every last letter again. I don't care how old they are, I want to read them. You don't know how awful it is going to be not to get any mail.
>
> This is a horrible country. I guess I am more homesick for you. I am feeling depressed.
>
> Love Bill

My dad was always "Mr. Responsible." I cannot even imagine him losing his wallet! This incident had to have been devastating.

Losing his wallet had to have been such a terrible day for him. He was lonely and isolated from his wife and family. Losing his cherished pictures would have been the worst thing to him. On top of that, knowing he wasn't going to be getting any new mail had to have been depressing. It was not easy to get Dad's attitude down. In fact, I never saw him low. This letter has to be the closest to depression that I ever knew him to be.

I can imagine how he talked about the Chinese jabbering! I was not raised to discriminate against any other races or people. Yet Dad did say some funny things once in a while without being a bigot like many Americans were in that era. When my kids were learning to talk he would say, "Those babies sound just like they're speaking Chinese. They are Jabberwocky."

I also have to remember that he was very young when he was writing letters home in 1945. His biases changed and dissipated as an adult.

My parents taught me to be kind to everyone and to give back to those who didn't have the good things I had. There was cautioning not to be extravagant because that was enabling. Yet be watchful to give in the moment to those who need it.

Dad knew people were different and described them as so but never as less of a person. Many people had attributes that he didn't understand. Yes, sometimes Dad got irritated when he thought they acted stupidly. He would never be mean or refuse to help anyone because of those differences though.

> He silently gave in small ways and gave big in other ways, and made lasting memories for many.

Talking to Dad later in life, he described the people he saw during the aftermath of the war and how that changed him. He realized as he aged the small things he could do to make a difference in others' lives.

He was silent as he gave to others. He gifted to some in small ways; gave generously in other ways; and made lasting memories for many. People knew he was a God-fearing man, not because of his preaching, but because of the way he lived his life.

Every Sunday in church Dad would only put five dollars in the collection plate no matter how much he had. He said he didn't trust that the church would give his money to the people he saw in need, so he kept it to share on his terms. I know this isn't the belief we all should have, but for him, he clearly saw what he needed to do and did it.

So Dad would use his money to help the widows and orphans he knew by just showing up with food or filling up a car with gas. Sometimes their rent would miraculously be paid, or widow's children would come home with new clothes.

Mom's sister was one of those recipients. Her husband left her for another woman. She had four little babies to raise on her own with no money, car, or a place to live. She would work all day, ride the bus home, stop at the grocery store, and carry home what she could to fix dinner every single day. Dad made sure they all had food, and the kids always had clothes to wear.

Dad never acted impulsively as an adult. You could see his mind twirling behind those hooded blue eyes. There was always the briefest pause before he spoke on important matters. He had a hesitation before taking on challenging tasks which kept him from doing damage to others or his family.

He would look at you, pause, then say something like, "Well, I'll be damned," or "Ain't that awful?" The pause was his way of giving himself time to determine what to do.

> We need old people to be the storytellers.

One such instance was when a neighbor tried to get him to gossip about another neighbor. The one they were talking about was a strange lady who had changed her name to "sheisme" (she is me). Sheisme was the talk of the neighborhood. She didn't have grass but was crazy as could be, and she mowed the dirt.

One day he stopped the gossiping by saying, "Ain't that something, she even mows her dirt. She's a worker, that one."

A silly thing he did one Christmas was to get Santa Dollars and give them to children from all over. I recently had one woman give me back one of the dollars that he had given to her children. She shared, "This dollar that Buster gave my children is the one thing we still put on our tree every year. It reminds us of the real meaning of Christmas." She wanted me to have it back so I could always remember what kind of man my dad was.

The artifacts of love are in my home. Arrowheads, Santa Dollars, and Petrified Wood which have no monetary value and could be thrown out someday if I don't give them a purpose. They would lay waste in a landfill with no story to tell.

We need old people to be the storytellers. The stories must continue from the early days. These stories help ground younger generations and give them purpose. The young don't even realize what is handed down to them. Somehow the family history absorbs into them without them realizing it.

Even in the most dysfunctional family, there is a nugget of gold amongst the poop.

CHAPTER 17

Slow Screws

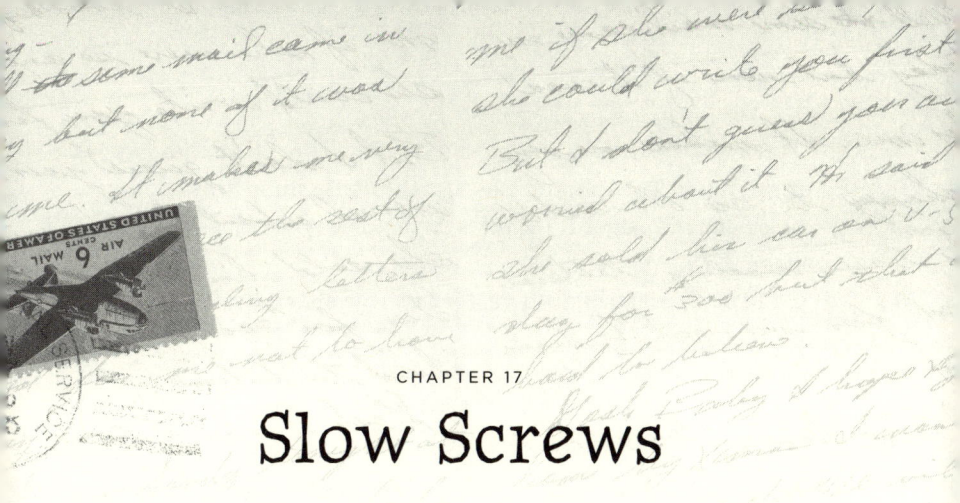

Sept 17, 1945

My Darling

Sugar I sure am missing you. You know when I told you I would only be gone a year? Well at the time I didn't think that would be so as an unreasonable length of time to be over here but if I have to stay over here a year, I will go nuts.

Darling, it hurts me so very much to be away from you for I love you more than anything in the world. No matter how tired I am when I go to bed I lie awake half the night thinking of you. It isn't' that I want to forget you but it always makes me so sad to think of you and I together.

My darling if I thought you wouldn't disapprove I believe I would turn to drink to make my stay over here more pleasant.

I saw a good show again last night. It was "Her Highness and the Bellboy" with Hedy Lamarr and Robert Walker, June Allyson. It was a wonderful picture. I don't know if it is because I'm over here or not but I really enjoyed the picture. It just seems to take me away from all this and makes me feel back home. I just hated for the shows to end.

You be sure to see both of these because they are exceptionally good.

"Her Highness and the Bellboy" and "Weekend at the Waldorf."

We got the "Hit Parade on TV last night at six o'clock, Sunday that is nearly a day's difference as in the states.

> We have a nice barracks and don't have to clean them up or anything. The Indians clean, make beds, shine brass and shoes and are general flunkies for us. The government pays them and we don't.
>
> I got my head shaved yesterday. It is short. I look funny.
>
> Bill

WHEN I GREW UP, he would fix us his drinks. Mom and her sister, Marcia, would have "slow screws." Everyone thought it was funny because it was a little naughty. The more they drank, the funnier they thought it was, and the more they would say the words, "slow screw," and laugh. The drink was so sweet that it was like a dessert. It was slow gin and orange juice mixed with ice. Dad would mix it up in the noisy yellow blender until they were foamy on the top and the ice got pulverized.

I can remember one night Marcia and Mom had just a wee bit too much and got silly. Mom said she didn't like the way it felt but she sure was laughing a lot as she said that, and then took another sip. Marcia would tip her head back and laugh, "Oh, Mary, you do too like how it feels."

Mom would say, "Oh no, I don't," then laugh and have yet another sip. Dad would cut them off before they got sick, but not before he snuck in a little extra drink for himself while he could get away with it.

Sometimes while he was fixing his famous steaks on the grill, he would mix himself a 7 & 7 and sit out on the porch as he cooked. After the second highball containing his favorite Seagram's Seven Crown combined with 7 Up, he was always cut off. I still remember the smell of the steaks cooking and how the 7 & 7 smelled. I can picture the porch, smell the steaks, and hear the door opening and closing as he went from the kitchen to the porch.

Mom would be in her muumuu bustling about the kitchen getting the potatoes out of the oven and saying, "How much longer, Buster?" He would come in and tell her five more minutes, and he would purposely kiss her and scrub his unshaved whiskers on her chin. Then we would hear her squeal, "Buster, get out of here!"

> Jack even took her grandkids out to drink with her.

His steaks were the best, too. He would rub them generously with vegetable oil on both sides and then all the seasonings would stick to the meat as they when on the grill. I think those 7 & 7's had something to do with the excellent taste, too.

It's funny that he knew the drinking would get in the way of their relationship even from far away and even at his tender age. He never minded her cutting him off, although he would sneak in an extra drink if she didn't pay attention.

It seems like drinking plays an integral part in every family's life. Good or bad, everyone has a story.

Dad's sister, Jack, even took her grandkids out to drink with her. It was no big deal for her to take them at seven and thirteen to her favorite club. After all, the club was where Preacher Smith played the piano, and Jack knew every person in there.

Roy Rogers' and Shirley Temples were the cocktails of choice for the kids. Jack would close the bar down and teach the kids to sing, "Up Against the Wall Redneck Mother." Another favorite was "It Had To Be You," which they sang all the way home.

As she dropped them off at home the next day, she would say, "You're gonna miss me when I'm gone."

> My life has been real pleasant
> I surely can't complain
> I've many creature comforts
> And some financial gain.
> —Ruby Lee

She was not lying. She was no ordinary grandmother.

CHAPTER 18

Hope of Mail

*All of the Cannon women were independent,
free-spirited, and just darn wild at times.*

Sept 20, 1945

Hi Darling,

Some of the boys got some mail today. It has built my hopes maybe I'll get some this afternoon or tomorrow. Darling I will be so happy when I do start getting some mail from you. I want to know so very much what you are doing and everything. It is so darn hard to go on not hearing from anyone.

    I guess you are working at the telephone office. Boy would I like to hear you say "number please." That would really be a thrill right now. I know you don't like working but it sure helps to know that you are busy and putting something away for when I get home. Just don't spend it all on clothes.

    Last night I went to see "Saratoga Trunk" with Ingrid Bergman and Gary Cooper. When the show was about half over the damn projector broke down and they couldn't get it fixed. The show was just getting interesting when it broke down. I was sure mad.

    Excuse the V-mail but I've very little time. I'm in Kunming to spend the night then tomorrow we will take a load to Shanghai and may spend tomorrow night there. I certainly hope we do. Maybe my mail is there.

This morning 3 men who bombed Shanghai on June 12th and were shot down by the Japs just walked in here from Shanghai. They had been walking since June 12th and just got here today. They didn't know that the war was over. They were sure happy to get out. This is a terrible country. Can you imagine, four months and they walked that long? Say Baby makes me feel blessed to be safe.

Well baby I have to go now.

I love you very much

You're favorite, Bill

V-mail (Victory mail) was developed by Eastman Kodak and was the main way soldiers stationed abroad were able to communicate with friends and family back home. Before V-mail, one of the only ways to reach loved ones was through Air Mail, which was sent by airplane and was often more expensive than regular mail and took too long to be used for any urgent messages. V-mail allowed for faster, less expensive correspondence.

> Each V-mail was equivalent to 37 mail bags worth of letters.

V-mail was one of the most secure methods of communication. Why? Because the letters were censored before being transferred to microfilm. After letters arrived at their destination, the negatives would be blown up to full size and printed. In addition to increased security, this method meant saving shipping space that could otherwise be used for necessary war materials. Using this small microfilm saved the postal system thousands of tons of shipping space, fitting the equivalent to 37 mail bags worth of letters into just one.

CHAPTER 18: Hope of Mail

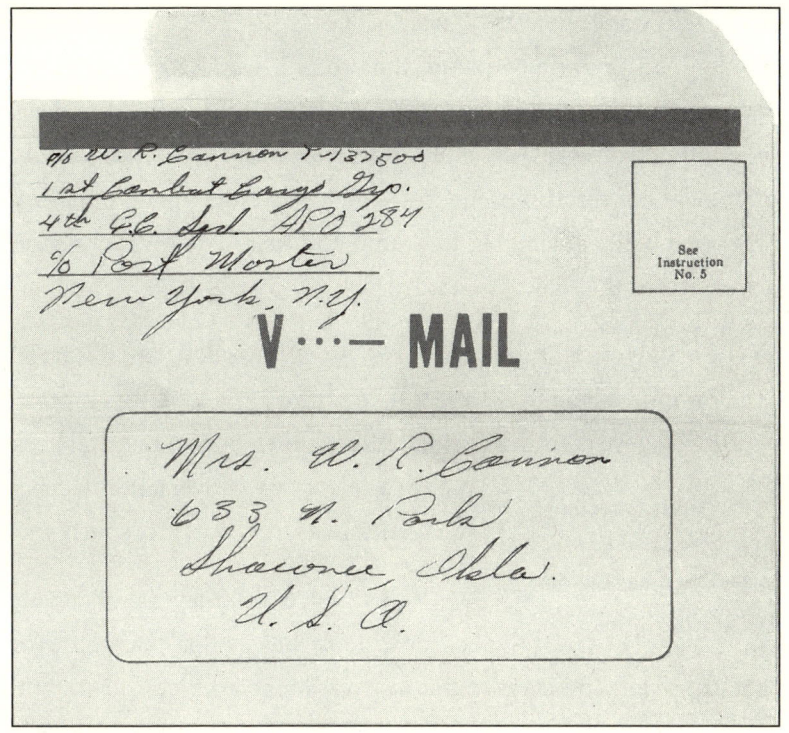

V-mail envelope.

Mom did work as a telephone operator while Dad was overseas. It is so foreign to people today that you had an operator who placed your calls on a home phone.

People didn't even have a dedicated home phone; they had party lines that they shared with the neighbors. When you wanted to make a call, you picked up the phone and often could hear other people talking on the party line. I can remember them (Mom, Aunt Marcia, Grandma) giggling quietly while they listened in on neighbors' conversations, covering the mouthpiece of the phone so they would not be detected. They were eavesdropping; for them, it could be very entertaining.

At the telephone office, there were a lot of cords that plugged into the phone line from one person to the other. It wasn't uncommon for Mom to become friendly with the correspondent, say hello, and ask how the person was before placing the call for them. Mom would often hear conversations and know all the latest gossip of the town. She loved being able to tell her mom and sister what was going on around town that day.

We have sure come "a long way, baby" from those days, but it is really kind of funny if you think about it. We have more tools for communication, yet we converse (to talk informally) less than they did back then. Now our conversation usually comes in abrupt, succinct spurts.

> In the end, the instant messaging leaves us lonely, with only a few words to warm our souls.

We use text, email, Snapchat, and many other tools, but we don't have time (or take the time) to have genuine conversations and learn from and about people. In the end, the instant messaging leaves us lonely, with only a few words to warm our souls.

At the end of her life, Mom wanted me to sit. She just wanted to visit. I didn't have time. I wanted to do brief texts or chats. She wanted me to see her, to hear her heart, and I want to now... when it is too late to listen.

All of Dad's family accepted Mom just the way she was even though all of the Cannon women were independent, free-spirited, and just darn wild at times.

Grandma Cannon had always worked in the home, out of the home, and outside in the garden. She worked in the shipyards during the war. Throughout the war, women—from all backgrounds and from all over the country—worked at jobs such as welding, riveting, and operating cranes. She moved to San Francisco by herself to work.

After the war, she moved back to Oklahoma where she took in sewing for a living. She could whip out dresses, coats, slacks, men's shirts, and just about anything as quick as you could blink an eye. She also knitted, crocheted, cooked, canned, and did just about anything to make ends meet all of her life.

One of my favorite places to play was her supply closet. I could stay in there for hours looking at the many hundreds of buttons, trims, yarn, and colorful materials. She never discarded anything. A worn-out shirt got the buttons cut off from it first to reuse in another garment.

> He takes all my money that I make, so I have to go into his purse at night to steal it back.

Grandma used to hide her money. She would say, "Old Dad is getting so stingy. He takes all my money that I make, so I have to go into his purse at night to steal it back." She would wait for him to come home from a wingding, then grab all the money that was left and hide it from him.

Cleo was the director of many communities while living overseas. While it wasn't a paid job, she ran staffs of houseboys, cleaning and building crews that built American communities while in foreign countries. Cleo did all this with the epitome of class, style, and grace. She treated everyone with dignity.

She interacted with her nieces and nephews as if they were adults, never talking down to them. She would speak to them about current events, news, sports, golf, and gin rummy; then teach them how to play. Her door was always open to family, friends, or her staff. Cleo opened up their minds to what they could be and achieve in life.

She was a fabulous cook; salads were her specialty. Cleo made a cheese sandwich, and wrapped it in foil. She heated a hot steam iron and pressed the sandwich with the hot iron. By ironing the sandwich it made a very thin grilled cheese which was to die for. I tried making that wonderful sandwich with my iron and ironing board. All I managed to do was make a big mess! No one could make a grilled cheese quite like she did. But one time she made her famous lemon pie and forgot to put sugar in it. Everyone was looking forward to getting a piece of that pie. A huge surprise awaited them as their mouths' puckered up, gobbling down the sour mess.

Syd ran the "Round Up" club and took care of most the rodeo events in the surrounding counties. She also bought and sold horses. On one occasion, she assisted Old Dad in the purchase of a grey Appaloosa in a neighboring town. Neither one of them could get the darn horse into the trailer, so Old Dad had to ride it fifty miles to get home.

Jack was a single mom and worked all her life. She was a salesman. Jack would dress up, put those high heels on, and stand on six-inch heels all day long. She could twist her butt as she walked in her pencil skirt and make a sale to men or women. Jack was likable, funny, and wild, very wild.

Even into her late seventies, Jack worked. Her son owned several furniture stores, and Jack was a top sales lady. One night three elderly ladies came into the store, and she promptly waited on them.

The leader of the trio spoke up, but she had a lisping problem as she said, "Yes, I am looking for sectional furniture." The problem was that it came out, "I am looking for sexual furniture." Jack, dressed to the nines, did not bat an eye. She quickly said, "Oh, honey, I can assure you that we do not carry any sexual furniture, but we have some nice occasional pieces right over here."

Ruby also worked. She was a controller at Rainbow Bread for more than 20 years. It was the only place she was ever employed, other than owning a donut shop with Wade in San Francisco for a short while. She would also sew, knit, decoupage, do ceramics, and even refinish furniture. Ruby always blamed Wade for her fat. She said if it hadn't had been for those donuts, she would have been skinny.

This bunch of women—my dad's mom and his four sisters—would try anything. All that had to happen was for someone to mention it, and they would try whatever "it" was.

These women were themselves regardless of the situation. They lived life to the fullest and not restricted by other people's opinions. The girls allowed Mom to be herself too; not insisting that she conform to their standards. They taught me to be who I am, all the time, and not let anyone change that.

CHAPTER 19

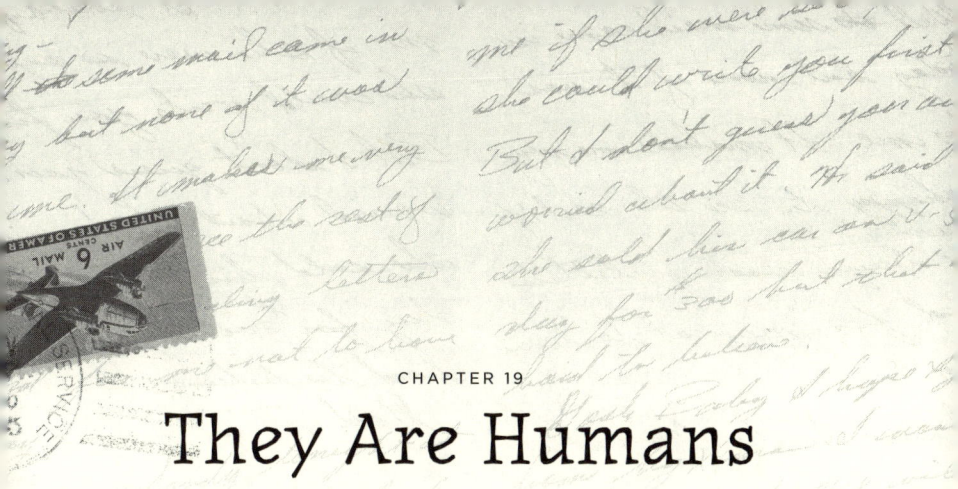

They Are Humans

*We saw a Chinese woman sitting on the curb next to him,
milking herself because she had lost her baby.*

Sept 23, and 24th 1946

Dearest Darling,

Well we made it to Liuzhou. Then we went onto Shanghai and we need a new prop now to get out of here. These crew chiefs don't know any more than I do about a C-46 and that isn't saying much.

I want to get back to Liuzhou because we might have mail there by this time.

I bought you 2 white silk blouses and one has lace. I don't know if they will fit or not but if they don't maybe your mother can cut them down for you.

Last night I was riding around in one of those bikes with the coolie pulling me. I saw a Chinese lying on the sidewalk with his head hanging off the curb in the gutter. He was groaning and crying. The coolie told me that the man had been very sick and hungry and that the Chinese would just let him lie there and die. They didn't care if he died.

Honey, they wouldn't let us help him. They said if we did then we would be besieged by beggars and that we could not help them all.

We saw a Chinese woman sitting on the curb next to him, milking herself because she had lost her baby. If I cannot help her and our country cannot help her, who then can?

I am sick. I cannot do anything. I will go back to our hotel room that is nice, with a soft bed, and with a bath, and close my eyes and try to forget.

I want to forget, but I don't want to forget. If I forget, I will be hardened. If I don't forget, maybe I will make a difference someday.

I just don't want to see what I cannot change. I don't want to keep feeling their misery when I close my eyes. They are humans.

My Love. Bill

> These are my "I don't understand it files."
> My pain in life and all their trials.
> The files that I must leave alone
> Or for my sins, I might atone.
> I refuse to carry the files with me
> Or let them be my enemy.
> I will not carry them where I go
> But forever my life has changed I know.
> —Lisa Cannon Reinicke, for my dad

> I've read til my eyes are worn out,
> And now I turn out the light
> It's a frustrating thing without a doubt
> To lie awake all night
> "Your guilty conscience" they always say
> "That keeps you from your sleep."
> You've danced and now the pipers pay
> What you sow you are bound to reap
> Its food for thought I must admit
> My sins are many and varied
> But escaping this insomniatic pit
> Might lighten the load I've carried.
> —Ruby Lee

CHAPTER 20

Mail

My big strong "Poppy" was dying and I didn't want him to go.

Sept 26th

Hello Darling!
I got some letters today! 2 from you and one from Cleo. Then more mail, 4 letters from you and one each from mom, Syd, and Jack.

I got the entire poop on everyone!!

I guess most of my mail has been forwarded from Calcutta. I'm glad it didn't go back to the states like they said it would.

It certainly was nice of Syd and Jay to let you all take their car to the city.

We're very lucky.

Your family has more company than anyone I ever saw. I'll bet your mother and daddy never has as long as they've been married spent one full week with each other. Although they were alone long enough to have Terry.

Say kid, since when have I let you voice your opinion as to the car? I am going to buy the car. I have decided that I want a Plymouth coupe like Cleo's Dodge. Now don't let me have any argument out of you or your daddy. I want to have some fun with your daddy over the car anyway! He thinks he is a car expert.

What is wrong with Syd that she had to go to the clinic? You know she hasn't felt good since Jana was born. She is a lot like my mother and yours too. All three of them can suffer in silence.

I guess Gladys is pretty disgusted because the Doctors couldn't find much wrong with her. She is repulsive.

I guess I'll write Gladys. I haven't written to her yet. I guess that is pretty bad of me.

Cleo got as good a deal out of her car as you did for ours. That was swell.

I can hear "I'll be seeing you" over the P. A. system. I wish they wouldn't play those songs. It makes me hurt.

You said you are having cold weather there. It is still very hot here. I just sit around and sweat. The flies and mosquitoes are very bad here. I hope I don't get Malaria but I'm pretty sure I won't.

So my little working girl gets tired at her job! Well you just keep at it and save enough money so when I get back I'll never have to work again and we can just loaf around and travel the rest of our lives. That would be nice but I'm afraid we would get tired of it.

I went to the show last night. It was an old Mickey Rooney, Judy Garland picture but I enjoyed seeing it again. Before the show started they played these old corny songs by Bob Wills. You would be surprised to know how much we enjoy that kind of music. We can sit and laugh and make fun of "Smoke on the Water" where if they played something popular it would bring back memories and make us sentimental and sad.

Baby if I were foolish enough, I could make 60,000 in three-years-time that is what they pay pilots for CNAC. That is a Chinese Airliner. I would have to sign up for 3 years and then the Army would release me. But the catch is, and the reason they pay 60,000, is because I don't think any man could live through 3 years of flying in China, especially during the winter months.

I heard today that we would have to fly 2,000,000 Japs back to Japan. If that is true I'm going to be pissed off (excuse me).

Baby I love you very much. I guess you are the best little wife a guy could possibly get and I'm very proud of you!

Well Darling I'll close for now and write my Dear Auntie Glad-ass a letter. Ugggg.

All my love, Bill

WHEN WE ARE AT OUR LOWEST, God can raise us up. Dad was indeed at his lowest a few days before with no mail, away from family, and then witnessing great misery. Today his spirits got to rise up by getting the long-awaited mail.

Oh my gosh, now I know why I say "poop" all the time. My dad was full of poop! He liked the word shit also, which happens to be my favorite word of all. I remember laughing outside my dad's hospital room when he was dying because I could hear him saying, "Well, shit."

He was the best-dressed patient in the hospital. Mom had him in clean pajamas every day that she perfectly pressed. She would wash and iron his pajamas even when they were just at home. His boxers were even ironed.

> He was in the bathroom, and I just knew by his "Well, shit" comment that he has just gotten some pee on his clean pajamas.

It was getting hard for him to get up and be mobile by himself with all the tubes and poles to maneuver around. He was in the bathroom, and I just knew by his "Well, shit" comment that he has just gotten some pee on his clean pajamas. I didn't know whether to laugh or cry; maybe I just did both. My big strong "Poppy" was dying, and I didn't want him to go.

Grandma suffered in silence too. I never knew of her even having a cold because she never told anyone if she was sick. At 83 she developed bone cancer, and she would just blurt out "shit" sometimes when she would have a pain. Even in those terrible times, Dad's sisters would get so tickled when "Mama" said, "Shit."

Mom's mother, Tiny, also suffered quietly with her brain tumor and stomach ulcers all her life. Never did anyone hear her complain.

I got a kick out of Dad stating that his Aunt Gladys was repulsive in this letter, but we were never privy to any information that made him use such a strong adjective.

> Sugar, your Aunt Glad-Ass is here.

Aunt Gladys would be at every family gathering. Indeed, she was quite the character. Gladys had enormous boobs that she would suffocate each of my cousins and me with when she hugged us. We hated it because our faces were always just that height to get the full impact of the smothering monsters as she pulled each of us in. I can hear her announcing herself as she entered the house, "Sugar, your Aunt Glad-Ass is here."

There was no missing "Glad-Ass" with her dyed jet black hair that was piled about nine inches high on her head—all ratted up. She had big, black glasses shaped like cat eyes with rhinestones all around them. She talked in a raspy, low voice, and called everyone "Sugar." She would make a grand entrance with her flowing caftans and "Hello, Sugar" everyone in the room with her low Oklahoma accent.

Growing up, Gladys was the sickly child that got the best of everything while my grandmother (her sister) got nothing. If there were oranges or any fruit, her mother would save them for Gladys because she needed them. She carried that sickly excuse all through adulthood. She would faint all the time for attention. She would put her hand to her forehead, let out a loud sigh, and then crumple softly to the floor making a gorgeous puddle with her multicolored caftans that she wore.

She had a house full of junk from all over the world, especially China. She would go to exotic places, buying treasures from other countries, and then come back to the states to sell them to stores. She brought the nieces and nephews junk when all the family got together. It was always something we couldn't care less about, like a pocket mirror or something strange that a kid didn't know what to do with. I remember she gave each of us a Chinese fan.

She had a mystery husband named Joe that none of us ever met. He was wealthy and had a plane that he used to fly Aunt Gladys into faraway lands. He died in a plane crash, but no one went to his funeral. I wonder what was actually in her secret life with Joe?

My cousins were playing in her closet once and found a bright red phone hooked up inside. They were messing with it when Aunt Gladys pulled it away from them. She scolded them saying,, "Never touch that phone again." That phone would ring every twenty minutes, but no one would answer it.

There was also a time when Aunt Gladys disappeared for three weeks. She left an emergency number for Grandma to call if anything went wrong. Grandma started to worry after two weeks of not hearing from Gladys, so she called the number. A woman answered and would not let her talk to Gladys, so Grandma said she was going to call the police. The woman said "No, I will have her call you back. Do not call the police."

Gladys did call within the hour saying she was all right. There were no sounds in the background other than a ticking clock. Gladys showed up at home three weeks later and would not say where she had been. It was always the belief that Joe was dealing in illegally imported goods.

Aunt Gladys met a terrible fate when she died in a house fire. Her house was where she stored her goods, and Gladys was a hoarder. There was crap in every corner filled to the brim. She would do her business from her adjustable bed with papers all over it.

The night she died she left a space heater on, and her house went up in flames with her in it. Death came as she slept in her bed, and never woke up.

CHAPTER 21

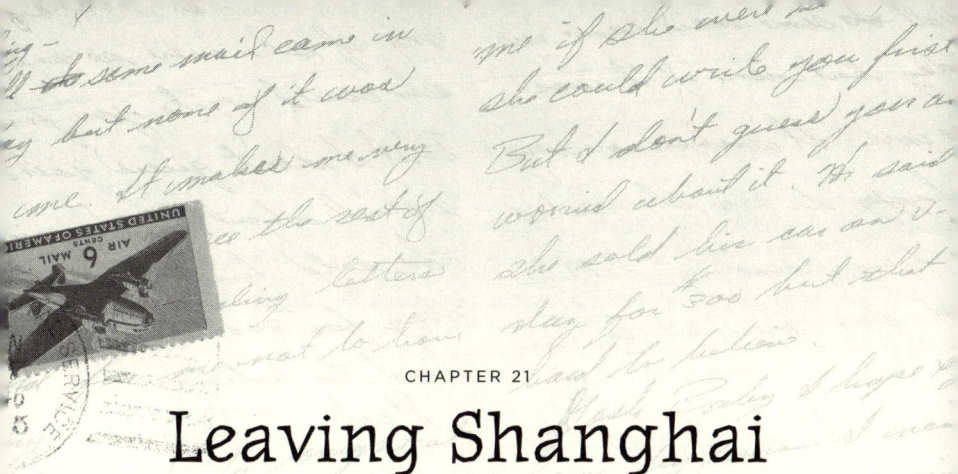

Leaving Shanghai

We are starting to move to Hankow tomorrow.
Ten shiploads of enlisted men will move tomorrow.

Oct 8th, 1945

Hi baby.
Well, another day has gone by and that means I'm one day closer to you. I wish this time would pass faster.

I'll bet you are glad you're working because you don't get as lonely that way. Have you bought any slacks yet? So you bought some new sweaters and paid 10.00 for them. You don't need to get too wild with that 25 bucks a week you are making. I better not come home and find we owe a bunch of debts. I'm just kidding you Baby. It's your money and go buy what you want.

Our food is getting a little worse all the time. Today at noon we had C rations, some terrible spaghetti and pineapple. I have a friend in the mess hall that just brought me some canned fruit cocktail though. So that will keep me going the rest of the day.

Hope I get some mail this afternoon. I wish it would come every day; I haven't gotten any more mail since that big batch last week.

I haven't heard any more about the Chinese revolutions yet today but I guess they are still at it.

I want to get me a camera. You can get German cameras pretty cheap. I want to be able to show you some of the scenery.

They just caught a Chinese woman stealing something out of a tent. An MP came after her and put her in his jeep. She tried to get out and he knocked her back in. I don't know what will happen to her.

I went into town yesterday and it was terrible. There wasn't one building completely standing. They were either completely blown up or partially blown up.

It was terribly filthy. The Chinese were lying on the streets dying and no one would help them. These people stand no chance.

I'm pretty disgusted today. This is one of those blue and dreary days. The sky is overcast and so am I.

I'm so darn homesick for you I can hardly stand it.

There will be 5 cargo squadrons of men and officers. The officers will live in one hangar and the enlisted men in the other. They must be big hangars to hold all of us. The town will be off limits to everyone. Some of the boys think we will have only 3 weeks work there. If that is true, I don't know what we will do after we have finished there. Some of the fellows are hoping we'll go home but don't get excited.

I will be flying and taking loads of C-rations to Hankow in my plane.

When I do get home I'll still be wearing these blue bars. The promotions are frozen over here. The boys who were up for promotion this month had to sign a statement saying they would relinquish all rights to go home. Promotion or points would mean that they would stay here another year. Nobody was fool enough to do it. We have 2nd Lts in grade for 2 years but I don't care about the promotion because it wouldn't even mean a raise in pay.

I'm in the officer's club writing this and there is so much confusion I can't think. So I'll say goodnight for now.

Oh my Darling I love you so very much you will never know how much it hurts me to be over here away from you. Right now it seems as though you are so much further away now than before. I can get along OK by thinking of our future but this is one of those days I can think of nothing but the past and the fun we have had and all we're missing now. Why does this have to happen to us? We love each other so much. I'm ashamed of myself for feeling this way because God has been so good to us for giving us those wonderful months and for not sending me over here before this war was over. In those days the boys stayed over here for a year and sometimes a year and a half. I just know I'll be home before then.

>   I hope I get some mail tomorrow.

The Chinese Communist Revolution or *The Second Chinese Civil War* started in 1945. This is the beginning to which Dad was referring.

Hankou
City in China
Hankou, formerly Hankow, China, is located north of the Han and Yangtze Rivers where the Han falls into the Yangtze.

> My days are filled with misery
> My heart is full of woe
> I must leave this cuckoo's nest
> But have nowhere to go.
> —Ruby Lee

CHAPTER 22

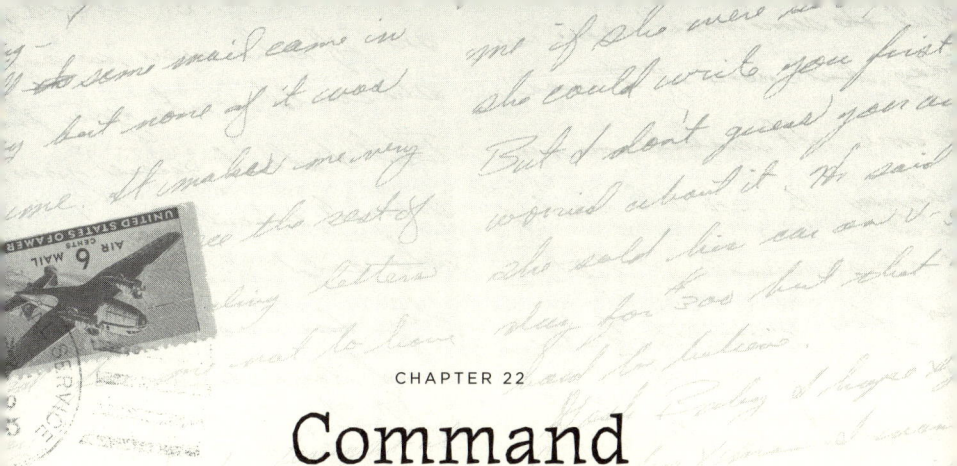

Command Performance

*I wish I could hear them sing again,
just one more song.*

Oct 15th, 1945
Hankow

My Darling Wife
Well I got moved up here yesterday and J.D. Guffy came over and we talked for a long time last night. He is an old friend of mine from home. I don't think you know him.

Well Guffy came by and we went to eat then I "borrowed" a jeep and we went down to the Jap internment camp and looted the place. We really filled the jeep up with Jap junk. When I got back to the hangar here I gave most of the stuff away. All I kept was a riding whip, spurs, helmet, horse shoes, and a bunch of pictures of Jap girls and their guy's family.

One Jap officer opened this trunk and said the stuff in it belonged to an officer and I could have anything I wanted. The pictures were in an album and I took them. I had a bunch but gave a lot of them away.

There is a Japanese cemetery about 50 feet behind our hangar and the Chinese have been digging the caskets up and taking the valuables out of them. The Japs bury the dead with their jewelry and stuff on them.

>Our living quarters aren't too good here. There are about 200 of us in this hangar. We have a shower and washroom outside but you never know when the water will be on. And you are afraid to take a shower for fear they will cut the water off while you're all soaped up. We have to stand in line for about 45 minutes to eat. Then after we eat we have to stand in line to wash our mess kits. The food isn't too bad when you finally get in to eat.
>
>We still haven't gotten any mail yet. That is what makes me mad. I know there is a lot of mail in Kunming waiting to be sent up here. There is no reason for it because mail is supposed to have a number 1 priority and we can't get it. It is hard to write every day and not receive any mail.
>
>We will start our operation from here tomorrow. I'm going to get awfully tired of living in this hangar with so many other people. I guess I'm lucky not to be in a fox hole though. But that doesn't keep me from being POed.
>
>We heard a couple of pretty good radio programs last night. They were command performances with Hope, Crosby, Sinatra, Shore, Langford, Hayworth, Benny and a bunch of stars. It was enjoyable.
>
>>All of me, Bill
>
>P.S. I just talked to the mail clerk and he said the reason we weren't getting mail was because they were holding it up until we got moved to Hankow. That pisses me off. Now it's not here either.

COMMAND PERFORMANCE was a radio program which originally aired between 1942 and 1949. The program broadcast with a direct shortwave transmission to the military overseas. It did not broadcast on domestic U.S. radio stations.

The weekly listening audience of military personnel was estimated at 95.5 million.

CHAPTER 22: Command Performance

Troops sent in requests for a particular performer or program to appear, and they also suggested unusual ideas for music and sketches on the program, such as Ann Miller tap dancing in military boots. Top performers of the day appeared, including Jack Benny and Frank Sinatra.

Daddy sang bass, and Mama sang tenor.

After seeing how many letters talk about listening to songs, I realized how vital singing and music was to them. They could share music, even though they were far away from each other just by listening to songs and knowing that the other one was listening to the same songs at home.

Singing had always been a part of their relationship; songs were essential to them. They would sing together in harmony. They did have good voices, and Mom loved to sing! Singing was in their soul and part of what made them a lasting team; they sang from the first day of their relationship.

Old Dad could sing, too. His favorite song was "Rock of Ages." I can still easily visualize him sitting in his chair on a Sunday morning watching church on the TV and singing.

> He was clinging to that cross from too much partying.

He would have his white dress shirt on; he'd smell of Old Spice, and be singing in his deep voice.

"Rock of Ages"
Be of sin the double cure
Save from wrath and make me pure.
In my hand no price I bring simply to thy cross I cling
Rock of ages cleft for me, let me hide myself in thee.

Another of his favorites was "The Old Rugged Cross." He had a baritone voice when singing it. The sound would make you stop whatever you were doing. It made you want to listen. His music was like a snake charmer's flute. When you heard it: you were in a trance.

Old Dad was singing for the atonement of the wingding the night before. He needed to hide himself after he'd danced his ass off the previous Saturday night. He was clinging to that cross from too much partying.

> Mom and Dad's singing wasn't always welcomed by me, especially as a teenager.

Mom and Dad's singing wasn't always welcomed by me, especially as a teenager. Of course, I was a surly teen; weren't we all at one time? I could snarl, pout, and just be plain nasty when I wanted to, and their singing brought out the worst in me. That first note would make the hair on my neck stand up and grow like a she-wolf. The second note had blood pooling in my eyes. By the end of the first verse, I could be in full-blown monster mode.

We had to move away from family when I was 13. All of our family and roots were in Oklahoma, and some family was just a few hours away in Dallas. My dad worked for Southwest Parts. Later on, Southwest Parts became Mopar (Chrysler). We lived in Nashville for a short time and then moved to Denver.

We always drove from Denver to visit family in Oklahoma or Texas. There was only one thing worse for a teenager than spending 15 hours in a car with her parents, and that was spending 15 hours with your parents singing the entire way. To top it off, they were singing church hymns!

That was one thing about going to the Church of Christ; they knew how to sing. The church didn't believe in instrumental music, so all the singing was a cappella. All the members of the church are taught from an early age to sing all vocal parts: soprano, alto, tenor, and base. The result is a four-part harmony that is beautiful to listen to, with multiple voices singing together. No instruments are needed or missed.

I was a royal brat at that age, so I decided the best way to shut them up was to shout out that I didn't believe in all that church stuff, and that we were all indeed reincarnated from something else, and they should stop singing about it. In fact, God probably would bring them back as ants so they couldn't sing. Better yet, maybe someone's big foot would just step on them.

> When Dad died, the music stopped; Mom's voice was never heard again.

My dad's response was priceless. He just started up singing again, "We shall come rejoicing, bringing in the sheaves" at the top of his voice with a sweet smile on his face.

When Dad died, the music stopped; Mom's voice was never heard again.

I wish I could hear them sing just one more song.

CHAPTER 23

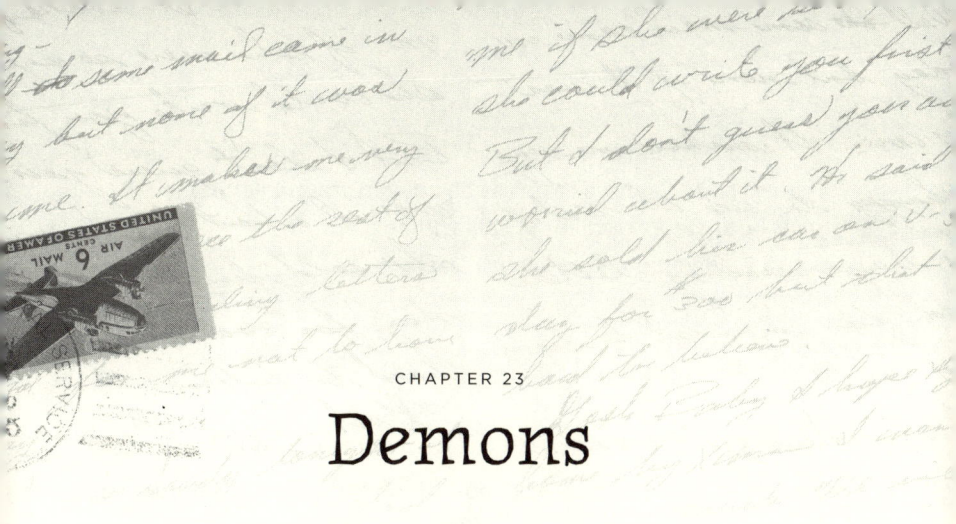

Demons

*They didn't act human because
of the strange things they did.*

Dearest Mary,
I'm sorry baby that I couldn't write yesterday but I was flying till 8 o'clock last night. This mail has me P.Oed. Irvine was at Kunming yesterday and they had our mail there but wouldn't send it up here. They said they were going to send it to Shanghai because we are supposed to be there in about 3 weeks. Most of the boys will go home by then. They will screen us out though and we will stay here about 4 months longer. I would sure be glad if they changed that though.

We have to haul 4,000 tons of Chinese to Beijing. There are 5 squads here on the project and with 20% efficiency they think we can finish the job in 3 weeks. At 2,000 pounds a ton that will be 8,000,000 pounds of Chinese. They weigh 135 pounds to a man and that makes 59,259 men. It is a big job isn't it?

We don't carry parachutes for the Chinese and if anything goes wrong we bail out through the bottom so they can't see us. We would leave them to go down with the ship but command told me that it wouldn't hurt my conscience because the Chinks don't seem like humans, they are like dogs. I hope we don't have to do that.

Guess who walked in this afternoon? It was Poot. He was the last person I expected to see. He is in our squad now. I think Sandy is in Burma somewhere.

It is cold here at night and I would give anything to have you to snuggle up to. Won't it be heaven when I get home? We will be so happy and all of this will be over.

I love you more and more Darling.

All of me

Pretty Bill

I HAVE NEVER, EVER, heard Dad discriminate against other races, although I had heard him talk about the "Japs" and the "Chinks" and say how terrible it was that he called them that in the war.

Dad said that back then the Chinese didn't act human because of the strange things they did. They believed that the demons following them flew in a straight line behind them. To rid themselves of the beast they would stand out on the tarmac waiting for a plane to taxi. When the airplanes were at full speed taxi, then they would run in front of the aircraft. Their goal was to run fast enough for the Chinaman to run past the plane. The plane was then killing the demon following them. Most often they would not get out of the way in time and the plane running over the Chinese. He hated those stories because he was the one piloting the plane. He could not get that out of his head.

Way back when, most families did not treat dogs like their children. And if you lived on a farm, dogs were fed scraps and didn't come into the house. The Cannon family didn't have dogs or cats. Grandma was not a dog fan.

The first dog Dad ever had was when I was seven, and that was because I had begged for a dog. So we got a little black and white toy poodle. Because he didn't shed, was cute, and small. This poodle fulfilled all the requirements of having a dog in the house.

CHAPTER 23: Demons   129

Little dog named Jobo.

Mom named the cute little dog Jobo. I have always joked that she was stuck on the name Jo. Her name was Mary Jo, she named me Lisa Jo, and then the poor little dog was doomed to be named Jobo.

Pepper was evil to everyone but John and Cleo.

This was Dad's first experience with a dog, and Jobo got treated like royalty. If our plane were ever to go down, Dad would make sure that Jobo was safe in his arms.

Cleo also had a tiny Chihuahua named Pepper. Her husband, John, was such a big man, yet he always was holding that itty bitty dog in his arms. It was quite a sight to see. John was a six and a half foot, two hundred and fifty pounds, pipe-smoking man, carrying a tiny little dog around in his arms like a child.

Pepper was evil to everyone but John and Cleo. He would be perched up in John's arms and snarl at everyone that would dare to come close. If you tried to make friendly with Pepper, his razor sharp teeth would get a good bit of you. Chihuahuas have a Napoleon complex.

On the other hand, Jobo was the angel to Pepper's devil. Dad now correlated dogs with being cute, loving, loyal, and joyful. The bad things they do like peeing on the carpet, rolling in the stink, or chewing a new good shoe, could quickly be forgotten when their little tails wagged and they jumped into your lap. Dogs were not valuable like the horses except for the feeling you had for them.

> **Horses were valuable to the Cannons; dogs were not.**

If the commander said that the Chinese were like horses, then it would have resonated more with Dad. He would have pleaded for parachutes for each one. Horses were valuable to the Cannons; dogs were not.

Kunming Airfield

The Kunming Airfield in southern China was initially built in 1923, ordered by regional warlord Tang Jiyao. In 1937, the Central Aviation Academy was relocated from Jianqiao Airfield in Hangzhou, Zhejiang Province, China to Kunming due to the outbreak of WW2.

In 1941, it became the main base for the 1st American Volunteer Group "Flying Tigers" (and later AVG's successor unit US 23rd Fighter Group, after the official US entry into the war). And as the war progressed, several major US formations established headquarters at Kunming Airfield. It was also a hub for military and supply flights to and from India and Burma. Shortly after the war, the US Air Transport Command (ATC) established an air route from Kunming Airfield to Clark Air

CHAPTER 23: Demons   131

Base in the Philippine Islands, which completed a worldwide transport route for the ATC. Communist Chinese authorities later converted the airfield into the civilian Kunming Wujiaba International Airport, which served the region until 2012 when it was replaced by the new Kunming Changshui International Airport.

Dad sitting in one of the training aircraft.

132 Buster the Football Flyboy

CHAPTER 24

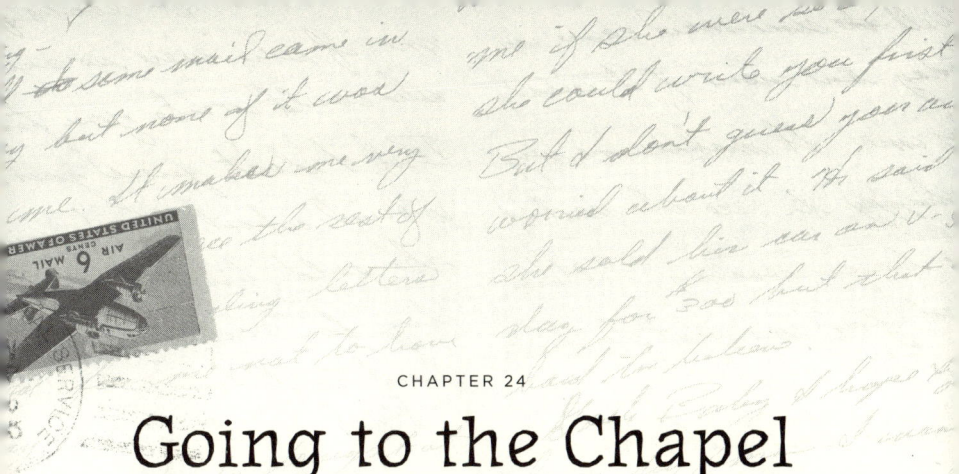

Going to the Chapel

*Only men could do the hard stuff in this world,
plus God sits on a throne, and that is where all men belong.*

Oct 18th, 1945
Hanoi, China

Hello Darling,
Well I'm still bitter today. We haven't received any mail yet. I get so damn mad when I know damn well the mail is in Kunming.

I was just told that a flight officer cannot get a promotion over here. That makes me mad too. There isn't one reason why I should work and try to do a good job over here. There just is not any reason for working if you don't get anything out of it.

I'm making 372.00 a month but still if some of these dumb people I know make 1st Lts and Capt. It just makes me mad to know that I can't get a promotion. I've told our adjutant that neither he nor anyone else need expect much from me and he sympathizes with me and said if he were in my shoes he would feel the same way. Sometimes I wonder what the hell I'm over here for.

Well I guess you're tired of hearing me now. I would like to change my allotment to 300.00 but I'm afraid I may be stationed where I'll need the money. I'm not going to accept my Oct. pay because I have enough now to last me till the 1st of Dec. I think. And by just leaving my money in the finance office it will be safer there than in my pocket.

I have 50.00 cash and 120.00 loaned out to friends. Don't worry sugar they will pay it back or I'll break their necks.

I'm sorry this wasn't a more cheerful letter.

All my love

                                                              Bill

---

                                                            Oct 19th

Hello Darling,

I decided to mail 2 letters together since I was so down yesterday.

Well Baby, I'm feeling a little better today than I did yesterday. I'm sorry about that letter. I'll try to write more cheerful ones from now on.

Something happened last night. I was passing by the chapel (Army Church) and they were having a song service—just 8 or 9 men and the Chaplin. So I went in and it made me feel something, especially through the prayer.

No it wasn't that I saw the Lord or the light. My mind doesn't run on that track yet. It was just that even though the chapel isn't the Church of Christ, I should go anyway. After all we all have the same basic principles and I can sit there and listen to things that maybe I don't believe and it won't hurt me in the least. And it makes me feel good down inside to be there because during the songs and prayer it is almost like at home. I felt like God wanted me there.

I talked with the Chaplin for a while and he is a Methodist.

So I came to the conclusion that I will be better off over there taking part in the service than here in my sack with absolutely no thought of religion. Sure the thought of how you were always there by my side at church will be with me but I can stand that because I'm thinking of you all the time no matter what I'm doing.

Darling, I'm so very fortunate to have you. I wouldn't be worth a darn otherwise. I'm so glad we're married because I can stand up under this strain better. I have a future now where I wouldn't have if I were single. Darling I promise to love and cherish you the rest of my life.

All of me

                                                             Bill

CHAPTER 24: Going to the Chapel

THIS LETTER ABOUT the Chaplin and the church connects so many dots for me. Growing up, the Church of Christ was the only church going to heaven. We went every Sunday, every Sunday night, and every Wednesday, plus I had Sunday School. This was the source of my rebellion in high school. The Church of Christ taught no drinking, no playing cards, no dancing, and that it was the ONLY church of people going to heaven.

The only instrument to be used in worship was our voices. They hung onto this belief due to scripture that said, "Sing and make melody in your heart." The singing was unbelievably beautiful to listen to. Everyone was taught to read music and to know which notes to sing whether a soprano, bass, tenor or alto.

> Our family ignored all of the DON'Ts that the church had.

This letter made me realize how influential the Church of Christ's hold was on Mom and Dad. If you were a member of the church, you most likely had been born into it.

However, our family ignored all of the DON'Ts that the church had. I was instructed each week NOT ever to share what we did at home to the teacher in Sunday school.

All four of Dad's sisters smoked like a chimney, which was not allowed. Dad drank beer, which was also not

> We would all surely go to hell if the church found out about our activities.

allowed. Playing cards and dancing was always going on around the Cannon house. We "mixed bathed" (swimming) right in our backyard in the homemade swimming pool that was a huge horse trough.

All those "don'ts" were "do's" in the Cannon clan, along with Old Dad's wingdings. We would all surely go to hell if the church found out about our activities.

I guess the thinking was that if the church didn't find out, then Jesus wouldn't know either.

Somehow I think Jesus saw Old Dad at the Honky-Tonk dancing. At least the Baptist preacher knew because he used to peer through the window to see how many of his flock were inside. But the Church of Christ preacher didn't go near the place. I think he was afraid he'd be struck down by lightning.

Jesus would not have wanted my dad to stay out of the chapel overseas. He wouldn't want him not to sing and pray just because it wasn't the Church of Christ. And I am pretty sure Jesus knew what went on at the Cannon house, too.

My grandmother was a Bible scholar in her own right. She poured over commentaries and had many reference books. I still have her large and very tattered book due to her extreme usage, called Flavius Josephus. He was a historian that was born of a royal family in 37 C.E. His writings are considered authoritative because he was an eyewitness to history.

Josephus documented the war of the Jews, the death of Moses, the death of Judas, and many other historical facts. Grandma would research the historical facts and compare them to the Bible so she would know the truth and all the facts to support it.

Her love of the Bible gave way to intellectual discussions by all the girls, their husbands, and Dad in the living room while enjoying pie and cigarettes. They would discuss scriptures and their meanings about everything, starting with God being a woman. The girls had a plausible argument on every topic.

God had to have creativity because of His love for beautiful things. He also had to be able to multitask to get so many things done. These facts alone must prove He was a woman.

This enraged the men, who argued back that God undoubtedly was a man due to the amount of strength He had. Only men could do the hard stuff in this world, plus God sat on a throne, and that was where all men belonged.

The discussions went on to talk about the disciples being men to which the women fought back that Mary Magdalene was a disciple. But the men in the group were just too stubborn to call her that.

The girls delivered the final blow, stating the fact that it took a woman to bring Christ into the world, which meant that without a woman, the world would be doomed to hell.

> ## To My Heavenly Father
> Should I call on you, Lord, to help me out?
> When I'm in a jam or need some clout?
> Should I thank you, Lord, when life is good?
> When I've worked and done all I could?
> I know you surely would agree
> I don't need to be on bended knee
> Do I close my eyes and reflect?
> Or bow my head with a stiff neck?
> Isn't love better than awed submission?
> Or confidence more comfort than confession?
> Good times and bad will hit us all
> And it's up to us if we rise or fall
> Please tune in with me and on occasion
> I'll share my life without reservation
> You've already given me what I need
> So don't direct or intercede
> I'll stumble and I'll fall
> And then to you, I'll surely call
> I'll rise and I'll be proud
> To never thank you Lord out loud
> I'm as good as I can be
> So please don't expect too much of me.
>
> Sincerely, Ruby Lee

CHAPTER 25

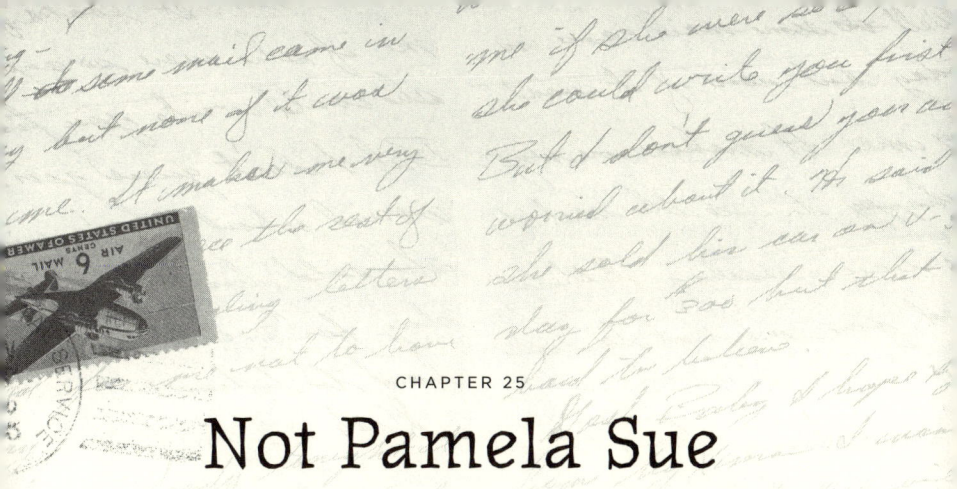

Not Pamela Sue

So Peggy and C. J. Hamilton got married?
Well they are a good match. Neither of them are worth a damn.
I wonder if they were both drunk when they got married.

Oct 20th, 1945

Dearest Mari

No mail again today. Darling I hope you are getting my letters. It is so hard to write day after day without ever getting any mail. It has been 2 weeks since I've had a letter and that is a long time, even then I only got one batch of mail.

I've heard a rumor that we won't get any mail until we get to Shanghai but I don't give up hoping that every day will be the day I can go over and pick up a big stack of it. I dream of getting mail and how happy I would be to get some.

I'm sitting here racking my brain trying to think of something to say but it is no use. It seems as though my mind is a blank.

Sugar, if I didn't have you to go home to, this overseas duty would drive me nuts. If I didn't think of what fun we will have and how happy we will be, I just couldn't stand it. I love you more than anything else in the world.

I would ask a lot of questions about home and your folks and mine and the kids, but I doubt if I will ever get my mail again. I know you are writing because the other boys haven't gotten any mail either.

Your homesick husband

Bill

P. S. Notice change of address again. Just keep sending mail and I hope to get it. Please don't stop writing.

Oct 22nd

Hello Darling,

Sorry I couldn't write yesterday but I had to fly to Peiping. I'm flying now too but I brought my stationery along. It helps me feel connected to home if I keep writing.

This is the first time I've flown 1st pilot since I've been over here. I have 55 smelly Chinese aboard and a full load of gas. I'm a little overloaded. The Chinks with their equipment weigh 163 pounds. It is a lot of difference taking off and landing a loaded ship than with an empty one. It's even more sluggish than a double glider tow and I've told you what that was like.

Well I finally got 4 letters yesterday late. 2 from you and 2 from Cleo. I was very glad to get them but I should have had more. I almost cried because I was so happy. It made me come back to life!

Guess I'll tell you the good news. The colonel talked to us this morning. He said we should have this Chinese Army moved by tomorrow. Then all we have to do is to move 2 service groups to Kunming and then move our own squadrons to Shanghai and from there, home.

There is a 50-50 chance that I will get to go home too. So maybe I'll be with you around the first of the year or even by Christmas. Darling that would be wonderful. I just glow all over when I think of it. If it does come true, we will be the luckiest couple alive. I'm still afraid I'll have to stay over here a little longer though. If I do, it will only be about 3 months. I would be willing to bet that I'll be home for my next birthday dinner.

So Baby, if I'm not there by Christmas, don't take it too hard. And don't send me any packages. Buy our silver instead and tell everyone else the same. If I don't get any mail then I know I wouldn't get any packages.

You didn't say if Syd found a place to live yet. I hope she did.

So Peggy and C. J. Hamilton got married? Well they are a good match. Neither of them are worth a damn. I wonder if they were both drunk when they got married.

So your sister is a copycat? She wants to name her kids all the same names as us. You tell her she can name her girl Pamela Sue but I'll choke her if she steals my son's name and I picked that name out, too.

All my love

Pretty Boy Bill

Note: Peiping, also spelled Peking, was the former name of Beijing.

ONE OF THE THINGS about Mom and Dad's relationship was that their gossip was between them; it never went outside of the house. They were confident that they could share those brutally honest words without fear of being betrayed. It was what gave them hours of content for their conversations. Hearing them talk about Peggy and C. J. is just funny because it gave them some levity to talk about gossip together.

It's funny how things turn out. When you are young, in love, and life hasn't given you a few knocks yet, you don't know what is in store for your life. In fact, even if you try, you cannot come up with the reality that awaits you.

> The perfect house turned out to be a few rented rooms here and there for a few years.

All the dreaming of children, their names, the perfect house, and yes that Plymouth, did not turn out as planned.

The perfect house turned out to be a few rented rooms here and there for a few years. Mom and Dad were lucky enough to find one landlord kind enough to let the young war vet and his bride use her living room.

They enjoyed being able to watch her TV and even had a few kitchen privileges. The young lovers could sit on the couch hugging each other and have those hours alone. Dad always had a cigarette in his hand, even as his arm was around Mom's back.

Being engrossed in their conversation, Dad didn't realize that he had dropped his cigarette until there was smoke coming from the couch. The more he and Mom scrambled to find it, the heavier the smoke got.

Before they could get to it, the flames had the entire couch up in smoke. Beating the couch with towels, they got the fire out before the rest of the house went up in smoke. The landlady that was so kind was repaid with a blackened couch.

> The new Plymouth turned out to be an old, used DeSoto that would start every other Tuesday.

The new Plymouth turned out to be an old, used DeSoto that would start every other Tuesday. This resulted in Dad's mechanical abilities.

That little boy they wanted never arrived. In fact, no baby came as planned. After returning home from his war service, it became their prime objective to produce a sweet baby to bless their union.

Cleo, the oldest, made no secret that John's and her lifestyle could not sustain a child with all their traveling. Her life was on the track she wanted, one of excitement in foreign lands with much to report to the family. Along with the jobs came wealth and exploration. Her secret was that she loved children and would have traded the money and adventure in a heartbeat.

She threw herself into being the best Aunt in the world. It didn't matter what she was doing; she would always stop to hug her nieces and nephews. Her huge, beautiful smile would let you know that you were indeed her favorite at that moment.

CHAPTER 25: Not Pamela Sue

One nephew stayed with Cleo and John while his parents were on a trip. On the very first day, he got into a fist fight while playing basketball at school. The other kid gave him a solid right hook to the eye while he was not looking. This blackened his eye pretty good.

When he arrived at Cleo's, she immediately went into action getting a snowball from the freshly fallen snow outside to put on the blackened mess. Then she kept him home from school the next day to protect his dignity.

Syd was able to have an elegant two-story home with two bathrooms, a large porch, and yard for the spawn she produced—one girl and one boy. She had the perfect life it seemed. Syd had a responsible daughter to love, and a son to be rough and tumble. But her enjoyment was cut short by a stroke.

Jack had one sweet baby boy, and another baby boy soon after that died. She could not make herself try for another child after that.

Jack never let being a single mom get the best of her. She was a great mom and went on to be the best grandmother that ever lived to her grandchildren.

It was not uncommon for her to drive all over town searching for baseball cards. She let the grandkids stay up until two or three in the morning drinking coffee when they were ten years old, while she and her lady friends played bridge.

If you wanted to eat cotton candy until midnight, Jack was down with that. She would let the grandkids stay up until all hours watching TV with her, although she could be found snoring more often than not.

Even Ruby was able to have a baby, which meant that she had to have had sex with "weird Wade." It was worth it because of the resulting joy it gave her. Her world was in her only child. It was what made her life worth living.

Ruby's life was with her child and then her grandchild as she aged. Both were accepted unconditionally, no matter what mistakes they made.

Ruby also had heartache. A pilot, the only true love of her life, left her at the altar on their wedding day. All the family, friends, and bridal party gathered at the church, but no groom ever showed up.

Running out of time, and desperate to have a child, Ruby found Wade. He was kind, unassuming, harmless, and able to contribute sperm.

With every birth announcement, it was as if God was saying "no" to Mom and Dad. They were asking for a child. They needed to ask to be parents for their prayers to have an answer.

Ten years into their marriage, despite trying, no pregnancy occurred. Hopeless, Mom and Dad mourned after every celebration of a baby's birth but hiding it so as not to spoil others' joyfulness. They would hold, cradle, and smell the scent of each baby.

Mom's sister did have that boy that Dad wanted, and then she had another, then another, and ended with a baby girl that she didn't name Pamela Sue.

Finally, the babies stopped, and it seemed that everyone had the family that Mom and Dad desperately wanted. Now at least the stabbing pains would stop and only leave them with the aching pain of desire.

That is when a miracle happened, me. I guess the family saved the best for last.

CHAPTER 25: Not Pamela Sue

Wade, the weird one, worked with a man who knew a young girl that was pregnant and could not keep the baby. Her pregnancy was due to rape. Her family had disowned her, and she was sent away to Wichita where Wade just happened to work. Her older sister agreed to keep her to hide her pregnancy. The baby would have to be given up for adoption.

Mom and Dad hired a lawyer and waited on pins and needles for the baby to be born. I was taken from my birth mom before she could see me. She never knew if I was a boy or girl. It was supposed to be easier that way. The hospital referred to this as a "clean break."

I completed their dream. Mom and Dad had finally acquired a home at that time, then a Plymouth, and now a baby girl. It was what they pictured. The name Pamela Sue was just a memory.

> I still recall that lovely day
> That we can all applaud
> Appropriately, a Sunday
> For it brought us a gift from God
> Evening was fast approaching,
> Four months of waiting gone.
> We wondered what the day
>   would bring
> We feared the plans gone wrong
> The phone call came that afternoon
> And threw us in a whirl
> For the news was that very soon
> We'd have our little girl
> She's given us something special
> A rare and gifted child
> Lovely and good but never dull
> And just the least bit wild
> This blessed gift and trust
> Grateful God gave her us
> —Ruby Lee for Buster and Mary

> To have a son
> Is lots of fun
> To have a boy
> Is such a joy
> But I get riled
> With my sweet child
> —Ruby Lee to her son

CHAPTER 26

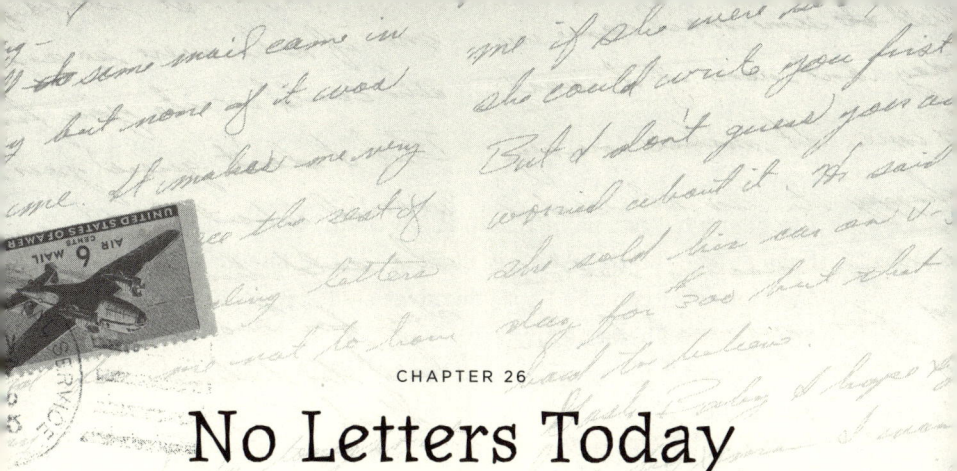

No Letters Today

There was no big wedding, mostly because there was no money for one during the depression, but also because it would have been impractical in both of their eyes.

Oct 25th

Dearest Marijo

I'm sorry I couldn't write yesterday, but I had to fly and didn't get in until late.

Darling I want to be with you so bad, each day it grows harder and harder to be away from you. Baby I love you so much. I'm the luckiest guy in the world to have you waiting for me. You are the only thing that makes all of this mess bearable.

We will really paint the town red when I get home. No, on second thought, we won't do that either, we will just stay to ourselves and enjoy each other.

How are you doing with your work? I know you are the best operator they have though, even if you don't like to work.

Be sure to tell me all the news and everything. I haven't gotten any more mail which makes me lonelier.

All my love

Bill

Oct 26th

Hello Baby

I wonder what has happened to all my mail. I know that I must have at least 20 or 30 letters some place and I never did get the picture of you and I bet you never said if you had sent it or not. Wish I had one anyway.

We aren't flying again until the 1st and then we'll go to Shanghai.

Baby, I didn't care much for A Bell for Adano" either. I thought that it had a very foolish ending.

Have you seen "Weekend at the Waldorf" or "Her Highness and the Bell Boy" or "Saratoga Trunk"? These 3 are the best I've seen over here. We have 3 pictures a week here in Hanoi and I've always seen at least 2 of them. It makes me so mad when they have a cheap grade show or an old one over here. They only have 3 a week and there are so many to select from.

Darling I hope I get to go home when we get to Shanghai. I want to so much it hurts. If I could just get mail, it would make it easier.

All of me

Bill

A Bell for Adano
1945 | War | 1h 43m

After the Allied invasion of Italy during World War II, U.S. Army Major Victor Joppolo (John Hodiak) is placed in charge of the small Sicilian fishing village of Adano. Though he is treated with suspicion by the villagers, his fair-minded rule of the town soon quells dissent, especially when Joppolo attempts to replace the church bell appropriated by Fascist forces to be melted into ammunition. While in town, Joppolo becomes smitten with Tina (Gene Tierney), a fisherman's daughter.

Movies did more than just entertain their generation. Movies gave them something to talk about, and they were a conversation that enlightened them to each other's views, beliefs, and personality. They fueled conversation with gossip.

Discussing characters, they were able to discover what made each other laugh, or cry, and told them about each other's heart.

Talking about the ending of the movie in "A Bell for Adano" revealed that they both agreed on certain aspects of life.

Mom and Dad's thinking was in unison, which enlightened their view of family. They enveloped each other's families as if they were born into each other's—all without a unison candle at their wedding.

There was no big wedding, mostly because there was no money for one during the depression, but also because it would have been impractical in both of their eyes.

> He told me to choose wisdom over impulse.

As young 19-year-olds, they went to the justice of the peace in the little town of Shawnee, Oklahoma to be married. The couple was deeply in love, devoted, and they were practical. Their eyes saw a clear vision of how they wanted their life to be.

When it was time for me to get married, Dad said, "It isn't the wedding ceremony that makes a good marriage. All the money that is spent getting married can be used for you to start your lives together."

> The end was as it began. It was Dad alone with Mom, their adhesive is broken only by death.

He told me to choose wisdom over impulse. Mom told me her wedding was better than any big fanfare because it was their time, not a time for everyone else.

With no family present, it was just the two of them committing to a life together. The family was celebrating before the marriage. Laughter, food, hugs, and happiness surrounded them as they headed out the door. The actual ceremony was just for them and would glue them together in their intense promise of dedication.

The end was as it began. It was Dad alone with Mom, their adhesive is broken only by death. The family gathered after their ceremony of separation. Their laughter turned to tears, hunger turned to fasting, and hugs became clinging to one another for courage.

Happy newly weds in front of their house.

Anniversary

The first year is always the hardest
Or so I've heard it said.
But brace yourselves, my children
For troubles that are ahead.
The newness now is over
It's time for deeper love
That grows with each new hardship
Each problem you must solve
So work them out together
With joy and selflessness
Believing in a common goal
Undaunted by duress
For faith and loving kindness
Unfailing tenderness
All the old-fashioned virtues
Will bless your soul with bliss.

—Ruby Lee

CHAPTER 27

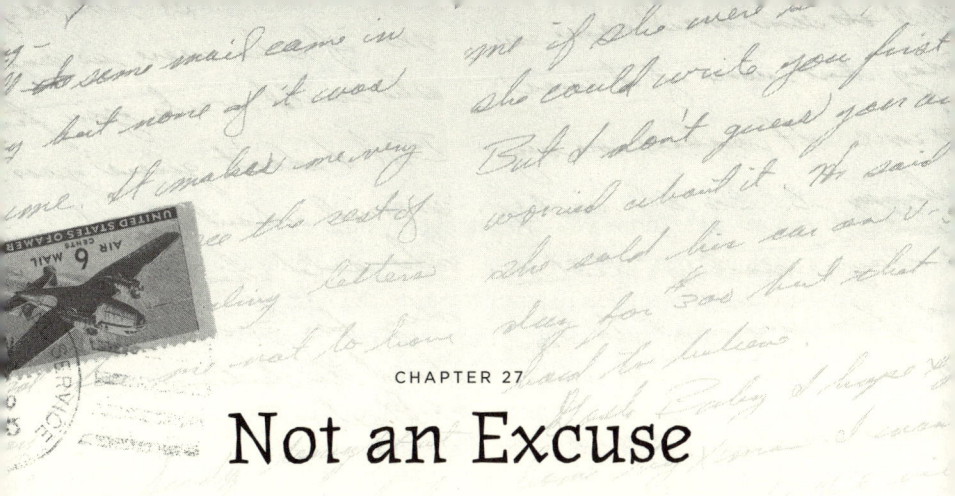

Not an Excuse

I pointed my finger at her saying, "This situation does not give you an excuse not to do the right thing and bury your head."

Oct 27th

Hi Darling,

I got one letter last night but I'm still wondering where my back mail is, but I am grateful for even one letter.

We are to be in Shanghai by Nov 15th at the latest. Boy I hope I get to go home with the old boys.

Darling it certainly is hard to find something to write about. We aren't doing much now. We have to be out in front of the hangar in the morning at 8:30. I think we will have to start drilling.

One of our ships took off a while ago and only had one engine. He ended up coming in on a belly landing. He was afraid to put her wheels down because he didn't have enough air speed and was afraid of stalling out. No one was hurt.

A damn Chinese pilot just walked by me wearing one of our A-2 jackets. That sure PO's me. I can't even get one myself and still they will give them to the Chinese.

When we leave here we will give everything to the Chinese. Well it is about time to go now.

All my love

Bill

Oct 28th

Darling,
Sweetheart I hope you are getting my mail. It is so hard to get along without mail. It makes you feel so blue all the time especially when you live one letter to the next.

About buying the car, I thought you agreed we should wait until the '47 models come out. They will be such better cars. And besides, I think we will dock in San Francisco but the army will probably send me to Ft Smith, Arkansas, to discharge me.

I know you look simply lovely in your new coat. And from the way things stand, I think I will be home in time to see you in it this winter. I certainly hope so.

I hope you got my letter telling you not to send the gloves. I don't think I'll ever get a package but that is all right.

Jay is all wrong about the income tax. I have to pay 36.00 a year and that is all. I hope and pray you don't do anything about it. I have plenty of time to take care of it myself. So don't worry about the tax.

I've got to eat now.
All my love

Bill

Oct 29th

Darling,
No mail today but this is Sunday and I guess that is the reason.

I meant to go to church this morning but we had to drill. We have to fall out at 8:30 every morning and drill. I guess the army is like that everywhere now that the war is over. It will be more or less like the peace time army.

They finally put the town on limits. A lot of the boys went in to town. I'm going in once just to see what it is like and that is all. I think because of the short time that we will be here; they should have left it off limits. A lot of the boys will come back with VD now.

Art, Scoot, and I are going to church at 7:30 tonight. I'm looking forward to it.

Darling I can't tell you how proud I am that I have such a wonderful wife. I can brag the rest of my life about the way you've handled yourself during this war. I'll bet Dad is proud of you to be working and saving our money and for not being one of those "cigarette smokers."

It's swell that Syd and Jay are looking at a place down by the drug store. If they get it for 4,000.00, they will be stealing it.

Got to go now.

All my love

Bill

DAD TOLD ME MANY TALES involving airplane mishaps that he and several of his boys experienced. It is incredible that there were not more fatalities or injuries that resulted.

He once clipped his tail in a telephone wire in flight school and had to land. When you think about it, these mistakes probably are what made them such good pilots. Dad was always one to think on his feet and to quietly figure things out.

He passed on this ability to me without having to say a word. The trait just rubbed off somewhere down the line. I learned that panic keeps you from thinking through a situation and wastes valuable time that you need to solve the problem.

These letters show so much about the kind of man that Dad was. A good man tells you that you are beautiful. Even when he could not see Mom, he knew she was beautiful in her new coat. A good man is faithful. He would not go to town because he didn't want even an ounce of temptation. A good man makes sure you are cared for. He knew Mom could not do finances, so he didn't want her to worry.

These attributes continued throughout their marriage—even to the end.

Dad was in the hospital when the doctors told him that his body was starting to shut down. His kidneys were starting to fail, his heart was giving out, and fluid was building up in his lungs. He was still very much mentally alert and could sit up to talk to us in his bed.

> Dad's power of substance is continually passed down as my children and their children grow.

He asked for his files from home so he could go over them with us. He wanted to make sure that I was there because he knew he had transferred his logic and determination to me. He had faith that I would make sure Mom would have all her needs met.

He went over each item in detail as I wrote it down. How much was in each account, and where to put it so it would grow. Where to visit to obtain his social security for Mom. How to sign off titles so Mom would not have to worry about anything.

There would be a time for tears later, but not now. Now was the time for business and logic. Just because we were sad was not an excuse for not doing what we needed to do.

I have had to use Dad's lessons in my life, and those experiences are so ingrained in me that they have a natural flow when needed.

My husband is an addict, and it had finally come to the place where he was leaving to get help. Our youngest daughter decided that since we had a family crisis, she could not attend school that week.

It was my turn to teach Dad's principles. I pointed my finger at her saying, "This situation does not give you an excuse not to do the right thing and bury your head. Under fire, we get tougher and more determined than ever to get in gear, and to make our lives better."

CHAPTER 27: Not an Excuse 155

Dad's power of common sense is continually passed down as my children, and their children grow. He continues to show us how to be a good person.

There was also another good lesson in this letter. As I look back on what Dad taught me, there was a saying he had: "You run with thieves, and you'll die with thieves." It was one of those sayings that I would roll my eyes at as I would leave with my friends for the night.

I can see now that he lived by that statement. Even in times where he could be made fun of for not going to town with the rest of the boys, Dad chose friends with his same values. Art and Scoot had his values.

Dad was always a good judge of character when it came to my friends. I had one older friend, Joe, who was right out of "Happy Days." Joe rode a big motorcycle, had the leather jacket, and even the hair of the Fonz.

Fonzie had not appeared on TV yet, so I am pretty sure Joe invented the character. He was older than me, but he was also a good guy despite his outward appearance. Dad somehow knew he was an OK dude.

Joe did some dumb stuff, like riding on the front lawn with his bike. Dad would come out and yell, "Joe, get that damn bike off my lawn, you dummy!"

Joe had this great smile with the whitest teeth, and he would expose it to Dad and say, "I'm getting off Mr. C." Then my dad would go in the house just shaking his head.

Dad loved Joe, and Joe loved Dad. That relationship meant that Joe would always take care of me; Dad's pride and joy. Dad

> Being a good person meant that you did the right thing when the chips were on the table.

knew there was something good in Joe and there was. He ended up a minister.

It was like that with all my friends. They were expected to come into the house, meet Dad, and be respectful. If they didn't come in to meet Dad and spend a while, then I was not allowed to be out with them.

The entire Cannon clan knew a good person when they saw one. Being a good person didn't mean that he or she was perfect. In fact, it said that the person was probably a little spunky and mischievous. Being a good person meant that you did the right thing when the chips were on the table.

Jack and Ruby found themselves in situations more than once that required instant evaluations of strangers. They were especially in that position one time in Las Vegas. Both of them, armed with cigarettes and drinks, were enjoying video poker.

Jack, twisting her butt in her high heels, led Ruby off to the blackjack table where more drinks seemed to appear. Drinks then disappeared before they knew what hit them. Reality raised its head as the time came to leave and their throaty laughter could be heard throughout the casino as they figured out they had no money to get home.

In search of honest looking strangers, they managed to secure enough money to get home. They got the needed information so they could repay the money. And they did—the following day, they paid back every dime to those kind strangers. That's what good people do.

CHAPTER 28

In the Gutter

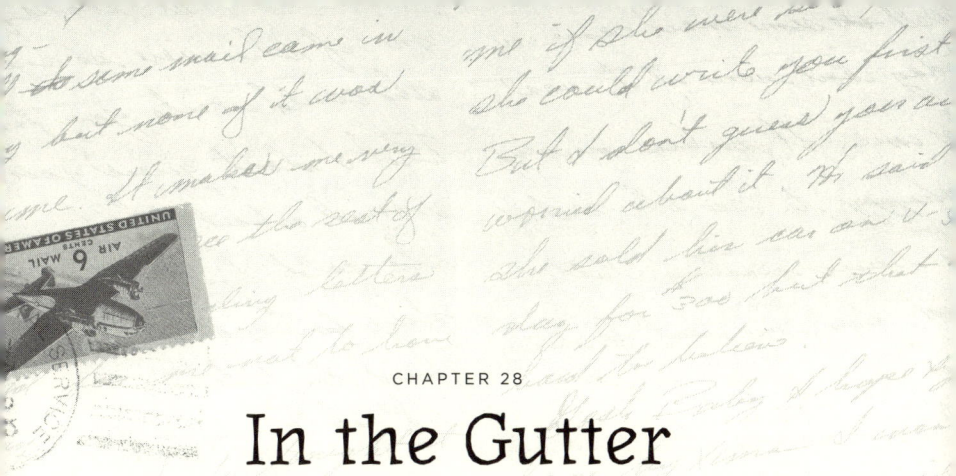

He taught me never to leave someone in a position that he could not get up from, always offer a hand to lift him back up.

Oct 30th
Manila

My Dearest

Art and I went to town today for the first time. We got in about 12:30 and had a fillet steak which wasn't very good. All the food in town tastes sandy to me.

This isn't much of a town. Nearly all of the best buildings were torn up. We had bombed them when the Japs held this territory.

The town and the people here are a little filthier than usual. They throw their garbage in the gutter and have sort of concrete walls about 3 feet high at certain points over the gutter so the people can go to the toilet there. Some of the people drink their own urine after going to the toilet. We need to help them restore things but there is not one person that can do anything.

The flies, gnats, and mosquitoes nearly carry you away. There are a lot of Japanese civilians here. They stand around on the streets acting completely contented while everyone around them suffers. There are a lot of Jap soldiers and they act like they are working but not very hard and not doing much at all. The Jap officers stand around like the civilians.

That is the only time I'm going to town. I can't look at what I can't help. I can't stand to look at the Japs. What they did to these people is more than I can take.

We will just be flying from here to Peiping doing I don't know what.

I am in the 322nd now. I haven't received any mail. I have just about given up getting any mail now that I am in the 322nd. I wish I could hear a word from home.

No baby I haven't heard "The End of Time." The songs that were new when we left the states haven't come over here yet.

Today is a down day, I am distressed.

I love you Darling

Your P.Oed husband

Bill

AT THIS TIME Dad would fly from Manila to Peiping (Beijing) which was a four or five-hour flight. He told me about how severely damaged Manila was by the bombings. He had a camera that took tiny little pictures. He came home with a cigar box full of them that were all rolled up.

The only way I could straighten the pictures out to see them was to get them wet with decoupage glue and put them on a canvas. I made a collage of sorts so I could get a feeling of the entire experience.

Dad continued his practice of not confronting a hopeless situation. However, he chose to face injustices before he would abandon them as impossible. He had a knack for lowering a person's defenses to get cooperation. He could then gather information and defuse the drama to solve the problems.

As the zone manager for Chrysler, he dealt with many people that were just plain angry by the time they reached him for resolution. I remember one such instance when a six foot six, 250-pound black man came in very hostile regarding his vehicle's performance.

CHAPTER 28: In the Gutter

Dad quickly took control by saying, "Man, you are one strong guy. Who in their right mind made you so mad? I need to have a talk with that guy." This instantly brought an uncomfortable situation into one that could be pliable as a result. A smile came across the man's face and was returned with a smile from Dad.

I learned from his stories and his wit. He had a Southern gentleman's charm and outspokenness that could readily be accepted by others because he was doing it with finesse. He didn't use big words. He didn't need to.

I learned to be tough, straightforward, and deliver it with a smile or humor, if possible. Give the negative news and follow it up with solutions. Dad taught me never to leave someone in a position that he could not get up from, always offer a hand to lift him back up.

I have to believe that the visions of the atrocities that he unwillingly encountered overseas forever stuck in his mind and would not allow him to leave a human in the gutter again if he could help them. He hated not to be able to help someone in need.

This is two photos Dad took of Manila while he was there. We have several.

We talk real plain in Oklahoma
It's a "big stink" not "foul aroma."
We drop our "T's" and maybe our "G's."
When others "grease," we just say "greez."

We don't sound pretty and we may be dumb
But we talk plain where I come from.

We don't confuse and frustrate
By saying dentures when we mean false plate.
We might even flunk our English classes
But we know that spectacles are just eyeglasses
Oh, we may drawl—we do talk slow
But our meaning is clearly seen.
You never need to go next door
To find out what we mean.
We don't sound pretty and we may be dumb
But we talk plain where I come from.

—Ruby Lee

CHAPTER 29

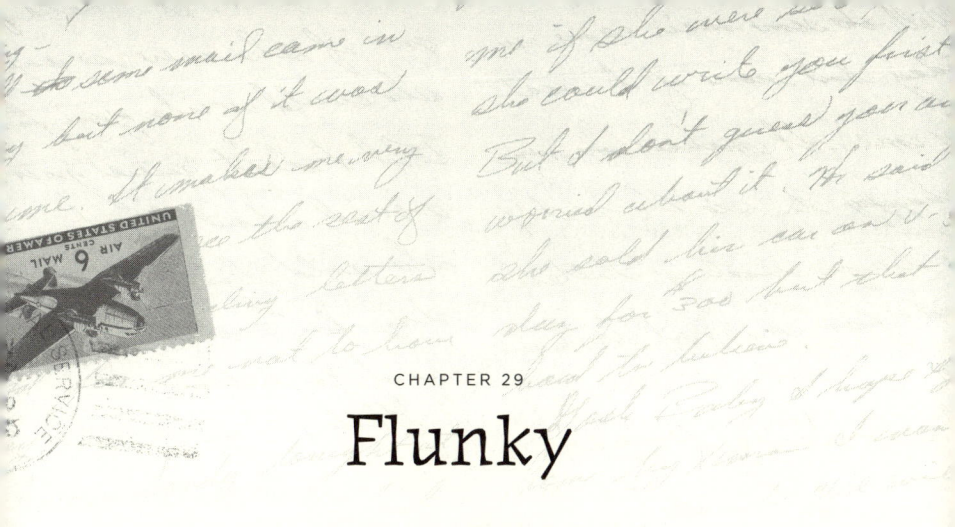

Flunky

I don't even feel like she is gone.
I keep expecting her to show up.

Nov 9th

Hi Baby

Well we had a little excitement today. It was about 3 this afternoon; I was taking a nap when I heard a terrific explosion. I looked out of the hangar door and saw smoke going high into the air and debris was flying in about a mile radius. All the glass was knocked out of our hangar and we are about ¾ of a mile away from the explosion.

What happened was a Jap ammo dump blew up. It was a building full of Jap bombs. There are a lot of old bombs left here.

The report I got was that 2 were killed, 3 not expected to live and 15 with cuts serious enough for medical attention. I saw the bodies of the 2 killed, but I would rather not tell you the condition they were in. I don't want to spoil your supper for you. But take it from me it was horrible. The hangar about 100 yards from ours has the roof blown off with an undeployed bomb in the middle of it among the beds.

The Red Cross building was across the road and about 100 feet from the explosion. It is completely gutted. There were quite a few in it but none were seriously hurt. The hangars there were being used as barracks and were torn to pieces.

My first thought was that the communists were attacking us. They took a town 100 miles north of here yesterday. I don't think they will harm us though.

I got 2 letters from you and one from Mother and Syd today! It was the first I had had from Mother for quite some time.

So you and your dad had a quarreling time? It is just like him to want to read your mail. Does he want you to ever show him your bank book or does he accuse you of spending much money? Those are two of his old traits.

Darling, my folks are really proud of you and so am I.

Gosh I'm lucky, I used to, before I was going with you, worry about my wife and family getting along harmoniously. You are truly a wonderful person to be able to please all of them.

You are a girl of relaxation by this time not working! Well just don't spend too much money because I'm a little worried about my earning potential. I wish I had more of an education so I could be more than just a flunky the rest of my life.

Oh yes, you will probably be sad to read this but I'm sure that when you think it over, you will agree. We can't buy a car until after I get a job making enough money for us to live on and to start a family on. Don't you think that will be best?

Baby there isn't any more to write. Tell me every little thing in your letter.

Everything

Bill

It's FUNNY that Dad talks about Mom quarreling with her dad being nosey reading her letters. Dad was the nosiest person in the world. If you ever left anything lying around, Dad would pick it up and start reading it.

I remember just getting married and Dad looking at our bills, our mail, and anything else we might leave lying about. When he was coming over to our house, we would make sure things were locked up tight if we didn't want them discovered.

He also made it a mission to call every night at dinnertime just to see what we were having for dinner. Not because he wanted to know, but because he knew we were eating and he was disrupting it.

That was great fun to him, causing me to get up from the table. He did this up to the day he died. It is one of the things that I still expect to happen at dinner.

> Dad's fear of being a flunky was not warranted.

Here is how the conversation would go and always just as I was about to take my first bite of food:

>Me: "Hi, Dad." (Because I knew it was him)
>
>Dad: "What are you having for dinner?"
>
>Me: "Roast and mashed potatoes."
>
>Dad: "Cream gravy or brown gravy?"
>
>Me: "Brown, Dad. Why does it matter?"
>
>Dad: "Just wanted to see if you were smart enough to fix brown gravy with a roast."
>
>Me: "Of course, Dad, there are no pan giblets to make cream gravy with a roast."
>
>Dad: "OK then." (Click. He would hang up.)

That was another Cannon trait. They never said goodbye at the end of a conversation. They would just hang up when they were finished talking. You never knew when the conversation had ended; they would just be gone from the line.

Jack carried that trait to her grave. Jack didn't want a funeral. She didn't want anything at all. Cremate her and then just be done. There was no service and no goodbyes per her request. She just hung up the phone. I don't even feel like she is gone. I keep expecting her to show up.

Dad's fear of being a flunky was not warranted. He was a worker and a good money manager. He was not a scholar but his common sense helped him work his way up in every job he had.

Once home from the war, he took a job at his father-in-law's dealership as a mechanic and selling cars. It was there that he was discovered by the parts distributor for Chrysler and DeSoto.

> Cash was his motto.

He worked there until they went out of business and were purchased by Mopar.

He then worked for Mopar until he retired. He advanced from selling parts to zone manager during his career. After retirement, he went on to work for dealerships creating customer service departments developing Chrysler's slogan: "Fix it right the first time."

Mom and Dad were not wealthy by any means but he always provided what Mom needed and most of what she wanted.

Cash was his motto. Only the house had a mortgage, and that was paid off by the time he retired.

I was an only child but was not spoiled. I wasn't an excellent student but like Dad, I knew how to work hard. He never offered college and I never asked. He never offered to buy anything other than that first free car. I had clothes and necessities; the rest I was expected to get myself.

Money did not get wasted. Instead, it went to essential items such as family vacations, Sunday dinners, or a special occasion. There was cash set aside and no credit card needed to be used. On vacation, we had a "pot", and when the pot ran out, it was time to go home.

No new TV was needed as long as the old one worked. Tools had an organization so they would always be found when needed. He didn't buy screws because he had screw and nail jars full to use for any project he was working on at the moment.

> There were no loose ends to wonder what to do with at the end of his life.

They ate leftovers until they were gone. Clothes were not thrown out; they got mended, yet Dad dressed like a million dollars.

He kept a register for everything spent in his "strongbox." He balanced his savings book regularly. Inside the box were his life insurance papers, along with his pension papers, receipts for the mink coat, and Mom's diamond ring. The house papers and deed were in order. Car titles were inside.

There were no loose ends to wonder what to do with at the end of his life. Everything was in order. He was ready to go. He had everything prepared for Mom for the rest of her life. She would never want for anything monetarily once he was gone.

CHAPTER 30

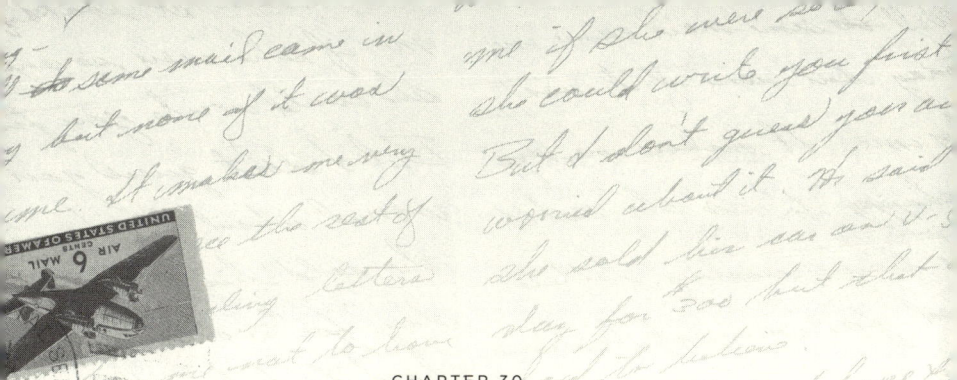

No Commentary Needed

He said he saw them throw babies up in the air and catch them on their bayonets many times.

Dec 9th

Hello Darling

Today was Sunday and we didn't get anything done. All the offices here observe Sundays and Holidays just like in the states. We are to report at the orderly room in the morning at 9 o'clock with all our records. We will have to take a 6-4 physical before we can fly today. One of the boys said he met a nice guy today down at the line and his name is Virgil Kums. I'm sure he is the same one we know.

I'll be glad when tomorrow comes so we will know what we are going to do.

Say do you remember in Austin when I liked "On the Atchison, Topeka and the Santa Fe" and you didn't like it? Well I heard that it was pretty high on the "Hit Parade" so I guess that shows who has the best judgment in this family.

We will be flying the brass this week. I hope that I'm not assigned to fly some big shot so I can stay here in Manila. This squadron assigns pilots to generals and colonels on all the fights.

If I stay here, I might get mail but if I have to fly brass, no telling when I would get back.

All my love

Bill

Dec 10th

Darling

Well we turned in all our records this morning. I will have to take a complete 6-4 physical in the morning because all my medical records have been lost. I hope I can pass it. I'm sure I won't' have any trouble there. I have a cyst on my wrist though. It is as big as a quarter but it doesn't hurt.

I got my tobacco ration this morning. We get 4 cartons a month. We get all the candy we want. They have Hershey, Milky Way, and Baby Ruth's. We get 30 bottles of beer a month and one pint of whiskey a week but don't get excited I will only drink the beer. Candy and beer, doesn't that sound good?

We have a boy named Pepi who cleans our barracks and cleans our shoes and 3 girls who do all of our laundry and ironing. So you better wait on me hand and foot when I get home.

Well that is all for now

I love you

Bill

Dec 12th

Hi Darling

I took my physical this morning and my eyes weren't quite up to par but I got through it all right. I've lost a little weight. I weigh 175 stripped. I guess that makes you happy. If I didn't know better I would have believed you thought I was a little too fat back at Austin.

They said the cyst is nothing serious then they dropped a big book on it and now it is gone.

We haven't flown yet. Our orders assigned to us have to be engaged in this squadron before we can fly.

It has been raining quite a bit the last couple of days. I don't mind too much though as long as nothing leaks.

Went to the show last night "of Human Bondage." It wasn't too good.

Darling I really miss you at night especially. The nights are lonely here. I can't begin to tell you how I long for you.

I told you I lost a little weight well I will probably gain it back now we have good food and all the candy and cookies we can eat.

All my love

Bill

Dec 14th

Darling,

Well nothing new today. It hasn't rained yet today but it is pretty hot.

I've spent about 50.00 on clothes since I've been here. I think I've already told you that I had to buy some khaki, underwear, and socks because these girls never got them clean when they washed them and they are so dirty they will never come clean. Also I lost 2 pairs of khakis in the laundry.

We stay as clean and neat as we are in the states. I bought a new pair of shoes today and a tropical worsted uniform. The worsted shirt cost 5.75 and the pants 6.80. I thought they would be nice to wear for everyday in the civilian life, if I ever get home.

My hair is long enough to part it now if I use both oil and water on it. If I don't use any oil it won't stay parted. It looks pretty nice if I do say so myself. Wish I were with you so you could admire me. "Conceited aren't I?" Of course my hair seems to get a little thinner all the time. I may be bald by the time you see me next but you will be so happy you won't care, or will you?

I wear a T-shirt all the time except when I go to work. I have to be in full uniform because there is so much rank.

We sure had a good meal last night. We had turkey all white meat and for dessert we had apple pie and ice cream. I'm afraid I'm going to get fat again.

My house boy, Pepi, brought me 2 coconuts this morning. I tried to pay him but he said they had 5 of them at his house so he brought me 2 and wouldn't take any money.

He has 7 brothers and sisters. He said when the Japs were here if they saw a girl on the streets and wanted her that they would drag her off to the woods and rape her. He said he saw them throw babies up in the air and catch them on their bayonets many times. It must have been horrible to have been under Japanese occupation. It is hard to think of the Japs as humans and not devils.

It is one thing to kill soldiers in a war but anyone who kills a baby cannot be considered human and they don't deserve to live. It is hard not to want to kill them for what we know they did here.

Pepi is good to us.

Pepi is good to us. Right: Dad in Manila with his new khakis.

I guess it is pretty cold at home now. Wish I were there to keep you warm and believe me I could keep you plenty warm.

Hope I get some mail soon. I love you more than ever

Pretty Boy Bill

CHAPTER 30: **No Commentary Needed**

MOST OF THE CANNONS never showed real anger and they were not mean. They were, however, very wild! Old Dad could be angry. He never yelled at anyone, but he could give the silent treatment for a very long time.

Being the oldest, Cleo was the first to get married. Old Dad was so angry that she was getting married. No one could figure out why that made him mad, but it did. It was his little girl and she had grown up.

He didn't talk to Cleo or John for more than two years. That didn't bother Cleo or any of those girls. They carried on like he didn't exist, allowing him to stew in his own juice.

> **They carried on like he didn't exist, allowing him to stew in his own juice.**

Ruby also could have a temper. Ruby was the only Cannon that could be mean. She was wonderful, kind, and funny, but she had a mean streak if you crossed her. She could say hateful things if you got on her bad side. There was a lot of self-struggling in Ruby. Things inside her tormented her mind.

> **"Wishing"**
>
> If you should have a job to do
> There's this that you should know
> You need a very definite plan
> Cause wishing won't make it so.
>
> It takes a lot of effort
> And strife and trial and tears
> To build a brand new image
> And mitigate those fears.
> But when you gain incentive
> Your confidence will grow
> The body must do your bidding
> Then your brain will make it so.
> —Ruby Lee

Fights were frequent though at the Cannons. When the male cousins showed up, there would most assuredly be a wrestling match. The winner would have bragging rights until the next family reunion. These events weren't out of anger, rather just out of fun.

After all the rowdiness there would be laughter, food, and most assuredly some pie.

I know I must keep going
I just can't figure why
There's nothing left here for me
Except to sit and cry
There are worlds out there to
 conquer
But my spirit is so weak
I haven't the nerve to try
Nor the heart to go and seek

Who has all the answers?
Not me I calmly said
Who has all the answers?
Not the living—not the dead
Most of us grope with anger
Through life from birth to death
Reluctantly performing duties
At jobs till our last breath
My life is one big anchor
That now I feel so bad
Boredom is the answer
Hopelessness is so sad

—Ruby Lee

CHAPTER 31

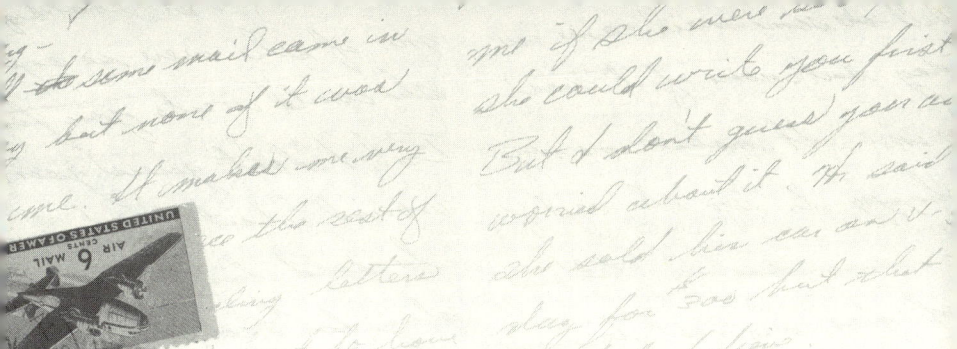

Japs to Dinner

What I learned from Dad was to pay less attention to what people say, instead look at what they do.

Dec 16th

My Darling Mary

I'm so tired tonight I hate to go eat but I can't miss that because I know it will be good.

Pepi took Wright and I to town this afternoon. Darling it is a shame how this town is torn up. All the buildings are torn up either by bombs or artillery. In all of them there are bullet holes where the Japs and Americans went house to house fighting. I honestly didn't see a single one of the larger buildings that could be of any use. They are torn to pieces.

Manila must have been a beautiful city because the buildings were of Greek and Roman architecture and were all painted white. Now it is nothing at all. The merchants have their goods and tables next to the sidewalk to carry on their business. I feel sorry for these people. They haven't started to rebuild yet. I guess they haven't much faith left.

I saw the church where the Japs killed so many and it was sad.

All my love

Bill

Dec 17th

Darling,
Well I still haven't gotten any mail. Baby you have no idea how hard it is to go so long without it. It is hard to think of enough to write every day when I don't have letters to answer. I can't think of much to say. I know the places that I fly back and forth don't mean much to you so it is hard to write. So I will tell you about the movies we see at night.

I'm going to the show tonight. It is George Sanders and Ella Rains in "The Strange Affair of Uncle Harry." I hope it is good.

All my Love

Bill

LOURDES CHURCH

STA. TERESA COLLEGE

Dec 19th

My Darling
Baby I really saw a good stage show tonight. It was an all Filipino cast. They were stage, radio, and screen stars of the Philippines. The director of the show is also the band leader and the MC.

The stars of the show was the number one stage screen and radio actress of this country and believe me, she is good enough for Hollywood. They had a baritone who was awfully good too. It is really nice seeing a stage show. We are going to see all we can when I get home.

SAN MARCELINO CHURCH

QUIAPO CHURCH

The picture show today was "Too Young to Know" with Robert Hutton and John Leslie. It was really good too. You will cry all the way through it though. Virgil nearly cried in it. But Honestly I didn't! You will enjoy it a lot.

Well Baby, it is late and I had better hit the sack.

I love you gobs.

Bill

I NEVER SAW MY DAD CRY but I can still see his blue eyes full of emotions that he experienced. He had pale blue eyes under his perfectly manicured eyebrows that were groomed every week by my mom, his darling Mary.

She would sit him in a kitchen chair in the den with a bath towel under it to trim his hair, his ear fuzz, and his eyebrows. He would sit perfectly still watching golf on TV with a hand towel around his shoulders. This act wasn't just a necessity; it was a performance of love between him and his Mary.

His eyes could show disappointment. Other times they could twinkle like dancing blue waves with delight. In sadness he would keep them hidden by looking downward as if he had to hide the blue color because you might see through it to find his soul breaking because of his grief.

> His heart broke for many people but not for any things.

His heart broke for many people but not for any material things. When he saw others with little faith left, he quietly went on a mission to help rebuild their hope. He knew that knowledge was powerless and that only action could give it power. Seeing others who were experiencing devastation was something he just could not let rest in hopelessness.

Ruby was one he could not leave in despair. Her marriage was cold and empty. Her weight ballooned to more than 400 pounds, and her finances bottomed out. Her home was in foreclosure and Wade was oblivious to it all. He was busy collecting empty butter containers and filling up the garage with them. In fact, to add another stress to Ruby's life, Wade had advanced Alzheimer's. He could not for the life of him remember Ruby's name.

Often Ruby would find Wade on his hands and knees in the backyard, watching ants. He could spend hours there in the yard. It was interesting to get on your hands and knees with him to observe and hear his insights regarding the ants. He would talk about the ones carrying materials on their backs to go to build their houses. He would say, "Ants don't waste anything; they can find a use for everything. They load many times their weight, they are strong, and that is what ants are."

> Dad quietly paid off Ruby's home out of his savings, which depleted his retirement fund causing him to keep working up until the day he died.

For Ruby, Wade's ant watching was hysterical and a blessing because she at least knew where he was. She would tell him to come in when it was dark. All Wade knew was that "stranger" in the house would have some food for him.

Dad quietly paid off Ruby's home out of his savings, which depleted his retirement fund causing him to keep working up until the day he died. Dad didn't stop there. He traveled every month from Denver to Wichita to not only visit but to stay and sit a while, telling stories to hear the laughter come back that Ruby once had.

Her letter states it best:

CHAPTER 31: Japs to Dinner

Dearest Bud,

I tried for weeks to put this in rhyme and could not. Glib as I usually am, this is hard for me. Not the gratitude—that surely is understood by you—but the real issue is more profound.

This issue affects several crucial aspects of my life:

First and foremost among them being this—you reached out to me when I needed you. I'm speaking of a gesture of love, not money.

When I wake each day, I can rise with renewed hope.

You've restored my sense of worth and dignity. Owning this house affords great satisfaction and security.

You saved me the embarrassment of depending on Bill, my only son. I am still mother enough to want to play the role of giver, not taker.

The depression I was feeling is changing, slowly but surely.

But the most beautiful thing of all is, you did it without condescension.

I love you

Ruby

WHAT I LEARNED FROM DAD was to pay less attention to what people say, instead look at what they do.

Shortly after Dad paid off the house, Wade died leaving Ruby alone but relieved in a way to be free of having to care for him. He was cremated and buried in a shoe box in the backyard, where their family dog, Sparky, was at rest in a similar shoe box. I can't decide if that is funny or sad. I can't help but think that maybe Ruby would laugh about it now.

Ruby's son married a Japanese girl. This union was a hard pill for Dad to swallow. Her name was Nancy. It was in the 1970s when the baby boomers were still touting free love, speech, and freedom of expression. Our parents lived through WW11 and were not ready for quite so much of those freedoms, mainly when they differed from what they fought for during the war.

It was hard for Dad to engage with Nancy. He saw the enemy in her eyes. Scenes of bayonets and babies floated in and out before her face. Her words never reached his ears; her kindness hit invisible walls keeping it distanced from him.

Nancy fixed a family dinner in an effort to show her love for her new relationships. Dad would not eat the food. He could not eat the food from the enemy. He quietly left with no words of explanation. That silent rejection hurt Ruby.

> She knew nothing of the atrocities the Japanese committed during the war.

Nancy was not the evil soldier from Japan. She was an American, born in America to a American father and Japanese mother. She knew nothing of the atrocities the Japanese committed during the war. She was just fixing dinner for her new extended family.

I will never know the discussions that went on behind closed doors that night. What I do know is that Nancy did fix dinner again shortly after that. Everyone ate the food, including Dad.

My Aunt Ruby died on 4-9-1997.

"Last Will and Testament"

I won't have a lot of cash to leave you when I go
Worldly goods that you could keep or stocks and bonds that grow
I bequeath to all of you my love; my greatest gift was laughter
Remember therefore with a smile and let the tears flow after
But with the tears—and make them few, think of me with pleasure
The happy times that we have known, have been to me my treasure
For all of those who've gone before and all who now remain
Made my life fulfilled with love that is all I want of fame.

—Ruby Lee 2-8-1997

CHAPTER 32

Done Is Done

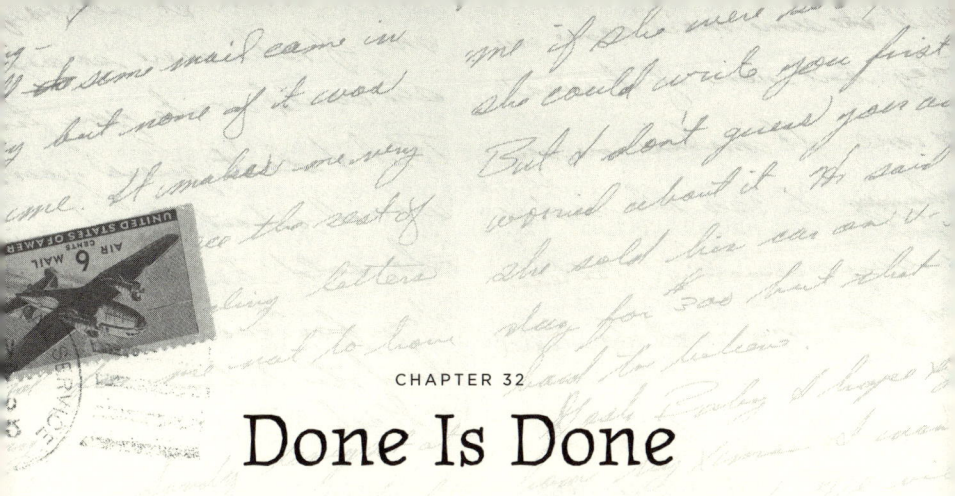

I do remember Dad talking about seeing General Marshall.
He was an idol and Dad did live by the statement
"What's done is done."

Dec 22nd

My Darling Wife

Boy do I think I'm smart! I got 4 more letters from you today and one from Mother. She said Dad named a horse after me! How do you like that?! Honey you don't know how hard it has been without mail!

Virgil and I flew a B-5 all day yesterday. We sure had a good time. It seems so funny to fly such a little ship. I over controlled a lot.

I'm so sorry John has been sick. It is probably from working so hard. I hope he is feeling better now and not working so hard.

Claude is in civilian clothes by now I guess. I'll bet he is sure proud to be home. He fought in this country and believe me it was rough. I can tell by the ruins. I'm so glad I wasn't in the infantry here.

Baby the reason I write the folks longer letters than I do you is that I only write them once every 2 weeks or so. I'm sure you understand that.

We sure had a good USO show here last night. There were only 7 performers but they were certainly good. All USO shows are from the USA.

You said the church was going to give Marcia a baby shower. Now you be sure to write and let me know everything she got and who all was there. I bet old Marcia thinks she is smart. Even if I don't get any more mail until I am home, if you write everything, I will get them someday.

Gosh I know your mother's closets are full now with both ours and Marcia's things in there.

Have you heard anything from Harold yet? I know he is home by now.

You better start telling me everything in your letters. How is Danny? Is Syd in her new home? I want to know how everyone is and what they are doing. It is wonderful to hear about everyone.

I just read the letter where your mother and daddy were both sick and I am so sorry.

Baby you just keep your chin up and maybe it won't be too long before I'm home.

All my love

Bill

Dec 23rd

My Darling wife,

I didn't tell you the other day that General Marshall landed here and spent the night. He is on his way to China to try to straighten things out over there. That is a hard job for even a good man like Marshall. I just got a glimpse of him but it was exciting anyway.

One thing he is quoted for saying is "What's done is done, don't look back but look forward and use the past for your next objective," or something like that. Don't cry over spilled milk. It is a good way to live life.

I saw Abbott and Costello in Hollywood tonight. It was just like all the rest of their shows, same old stuff. They are sure dumb.

Last night at the club they had a floor show and it was pretty good. All Filipino talent. One was a 14 year old girl who sang and she was terrific. She had a voice like a grown person and performed like a professional. These people are certainly musically inclined.

I try to keep from writing about how much I love and miss you because it makes both of us feel bad if I write about it all the time. Being lonely is humbling.

Always

Bill

I DO REMEMBER DAD talking about seeing General Marshall. He was an idol of his and Dad did live by the statement "what's done is done."

He didn't always talk about it in those terms but it was the way he handled situations. Words were not Dad's first language. He used actions, or the lack of actions, whichever fit the circumstances.

I never feared the wrath of my dad. I feared the lack of wrath because I knew that what was done—was done, but my future would be severely impacted.

Dad worked at Chrysler Corp as a zone manager most of his life. He had all the Denver car dealerships in his region. On my 16th birthday, he purchased me a used car from one of his dealerships. It was an old Dodge Dart with push buttons on the dash for drive, reverse, and park.

> It called my name—begging me to visit.

I still remember how it sounded as I would push the big rectangular button marked drive. The buttons were not easy to push, and each made a click as it put the car into a gear.

I was not an experienced driver. Knowing this, my parents put boundaries in place giving me a circle of roads I could travel. I was allowed to go roughly five miles in any direction, but I was not permitted to enter the next town.

The A&W drive-in was where everyone would meet up and hang out. This was not within that circle but was within my desire. It called my name—begging me to visit. Two weeks into my new driving experience, I broke my boundary rules. With my heart racing, I drove around that A&W, and what a great thrill it was.

I was sixteen and officially an adult, doing adult things. I was driving where I wanted with my best friend in the car. While driving, I was smoking a fine cigarette, which I had positioned elegantly between my fingers on the steering wheel. The boys were checking us both out and I knew they must be thinking we were older than we were.

That is when fate decided to throw me a curve because I was a little too full of myself. I turned my head to check out the boys in the lane next to to me. I didn't see a Jeep parked on the other side. I hit it full on.

I still remember the eerie silence that came after the crash. Then the accident became a reality and sounds of help started arriving. That still silence seemed to last an eternity, yet lasted only seconds.

I had minor injuries and I had bitten through my lip, but thankfully no one was seriously hurt. However being wounded was not the first thing on my mind. I was thinking about the cigarette, and my parents finding out that I smoked. My immediate response was to empty the ashtray before my parents arrived. After I accomplished that task, I noticed the blood and my lip hanging loose.

> **I went from hero to zero in 60 seconds.**

That incident was not spoken of by my dad other than he was grateful I was not hurt any worse. He did not mention that I was in a place I should not have been. He didn't talk about the smoking that he knew was going on, or what would be my punishment for the offenses. What was done was done.

I knew there would be no other car to replace the Dart. I would not have to worry about being where I shouldn't be because there was no way to get there. And my money supply was no longer available for cigarettes. To top it all off, there would be no sympathy for my lip whatsoever. The scar would be there to remind me of the importance of my actions. The cute boys that were in the car next to us were long gone, and probably having a good laugh that I was so stupid. I went from hero to zero in 60 seconds.

Dad needed no words; he never did.

184 Buster the Football Flyboy

CHAPTER 33

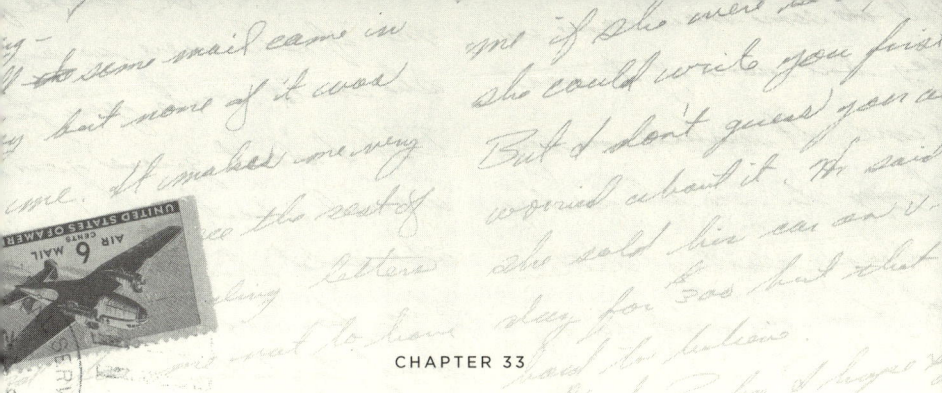

It Doesn't Seem Like Christmas

The kids got toy cannon that shot real cannonballs on Christmas. We also had toy guns and other harmful toys that were appropriate back in the day.

Dec 24th, 1945

My Darling Mary

I got another letter from you written on the 3rd. I wonder what happened to the ones written between the 29th and the 3rd? I'll probably never get them. I must have hundreds of letters somewhere.

You had been sick when you wrote this one and I hope you are better by now. I know how often you have to vomit when you're sick at your stomach. I'm glad I don't' have that trouble.

I would like to see Syd and Jay's new home. What does Jana think of it, a big house like that with an upstairs and everything?

Darling I've been so lonesome for you today. It has been raining all day and I've been in bed reading. I finished one of the books I bought and I certainly enjoyed it. But no matter how interesting a book is, I still want to come home all the time.

It seems like when it is raining, I am more lonesome and I don't know why. It may be the pelting of the drops on the tin roof or it may be that it is so dark and dreary out. I have been humbled because I think a lot about life here.

Say did you ever send me a picture that we had made while we were home the last time? If you did I haven't received it yet. I hope you didn't send a big one and it's lost.

Say Baby, send me a financial statement. Exactly how much we have in the bank and everything spent. I'm getting a little worried about the future. I hope I can find a decent job. That is why it is so important for us to save now.

All my love

Bill

Dec 25th, 1945 Christmas

My Darling Mary,

I can truthfully say that this is a very un-Christian atmosphere. It isn't the least bit cold and we have no decorations in our house. I thought a lot of the boys would be drunk today but none of them are. They drank a little last night though.

Now Darling, I want you to tell me all about what happened at home. I want to know who all was at your house and I want to know exactly what they got. And when you had the tree at my house what all did Gary and Jana say and do? I want to know what all the kids got and let me know what you bought yourself for Christmas.

We had a nice dinner today. We had turkey with dressing, potatoes, pickles, asparagus, peas, coffee, hard candy, nuts, and raisin pie. I'm sure they are having a show tonight so I can do something too.

The laundry girls made me promise to buy them some candy tomorrow for their present. Now don't get the wrong idea, they are only about 14 years old and I'm still quite respectable and very much in love with you.

I'm not much more lonesome today than any other day because it really doesn't feel like Christmas. I keep thinking about last Christmas and instead think of all the future Christmas's we will have. I sure will enjoy the holidays of 1946 better than this year.

I adore you

Bill

CHAPTER 33: It Doesn't Seem Like Christmas

I LOVED CHRISTMAS AND I STILL DO. Yes, there was delight in opening all the presents that I would get, but there was so much more. With the Cannons, it was crazy, fun, and meaningful.

Leading up to the event of Christmas, we had to prepare. Dad would deliver the toys I would sacrifice across the railroad tracks to the poor town where Gaines and his family lived. He would be invited in to sit and chat. He believed that time together with Gaines was as important as the gifts he was delivering. He enhanced every activity with good manners and taught me the same.

> **I learned not to judge people that had less than me.**

I learned not to judge people that had less than me. Money did not make the man. You could learn the true character of a person by the way he treated his family and those around him.

Next item up on the Christmas agenda was selecting and preparing the tree. We never had a full tree; it was always sort of sparse when it came to branches. Dad wanted to leave room for decorations.

First the lights were tested and attached followed by the old glass bulbs. Typically a few bulbs would break, splintering glass all over. And finally it was the time to hang the tinsel. It was a time-consuming task but we were not allowed to put the tinsel on in clumps. Instead, we would have to put it on the tree one or two strands at a time. I can still remember pulling out the silvery strands from the box and draping them over the tips of the branches near the lights so that they would glisten.

Shopping for others came before asking Santa for anything. Dad took me to the dime store with my change jar in hand to buy for people on my list. This instilled in me that giving indeed was more fun than receiving. Watching others open their gifts was more fun than opening gifts I received.

As a child, we always went to Mom's side of the family on Christmas Eve. I can remember waiting for all the mothers to clean the kitchen. My mom's side of the family was proper and dignified. Things were done orderly.

After cleaning the kitchen, we waited even longer for them to fix their makeup. The wait was excruciatingly long. The women would have to do lipstick, powder, and hair before we could open a single present.

By this time the children were out of control with excitement, even doing cartwheels in the living room. Every one of us would be yelling and screaming: "Hurry up! How much longer?"

On Christmas morning Santa came with just a few select gifts. That special time was set aside for the quiet of our family.

> **Christmas night was the wild time with Dad's side of the family.**

Christmas night was the wild time with Dad's side of the family. Each Christmas brought its own uniqueness. Every year there was at least one homemade gift from Grandma. Many wonderful things came out of her magical sewing closet.

All of my dolls would get a treasure chest full of new clothes. Along with them would be dresses for me that matched my dolls. Knitted sweaters might be among the presents, and slippers for every person.

One year she made all the kids human-sized dolls using flesh-colored cloth and stuffed them. She dressed the dolls in our clothes. This created a fascinating outcome that I'm sure Grandma didn't expect. The boys used the dolls as a boxing partner while the girls were all about loving their dolls.

CHAPTER 33: It Doesn't Seem Like Christmas

Jana was Syd's oldest daughter and Gary was Jack's son. They were the same age and always the leaders at the Cannon Christmas party. Jana was responsible and Gary was not. These two lead all the kids for a Christmas fight upstairs at Aunt Syd's house.

One of the intelligent adults gave us a toy cannon that shot real cannonballs on Christmas. We also had toy guns and other harmful toys that were appropriate back in the day. We decided a war was in order and our battleground was the upstairs den.

Jana voted for safety making sure all the pillows in the house were piled up to protect both sides. Gary concentrated on ammunition for a great fight. We were loud, we made a mess, and we lived through it.

Syd never cared about the mess we made; it could be cleaned up. She never told us to be quiet; happy noise was always welcome. When there was crying, Syd checked for blood and broken bones. If there was none, she gave a kiss, a pat, and a laugh and sent us on our way.

The house that Dad talks about Syd and Jay getting was a mansion for those days. It was a big two story with several living areas for congregating. The Cannon clan was good at assembling en mass. There was red felt wallpaper that went all the way up the wall of the stairway. Every child rubbed

> He was taken out to the yard and hung on the clothesline upside down.

the felt each time we went up or down the stairs. I am sure it was threadbare from all the little hands continually touching it, but Syd never told us to get our hands off the wall.

Jay was J. C. Robb and he was tortured by the Cannon clan when he first married Syd. He was taken out to the yard and hung on the clothesline upside down. Then they left him there yelling to get undone. It was the girls that saved him. An initiation into the Cannons meant that you were a Cannon for life.

Syd had a stroke when she was only 50, which was not surprising since each of Dad's four sisters smoked one cigarette after another. A new one would be lit off the one they had just finished.

I remember her sitting in her chair, but her laughter was quiet as the stroke took her joy also. It was a harsh sentence to endure for someone so ordinarily full of adventure. Vesta Lavern (Syd) died at 57, but she would never go away for the ones that hold her spirit in their hearts.

> ### "Holidays"
> I tell you the truth
> I got to confess
> Those holidays are just
> A big damn mess.
> I revert to the days
> When I was young
> And families together
> Were so much fun.
> I strive to remember,
> Traditions of old
> But those strange customs
> Just leave them cold.
> I fix the dinner
> They get here late
> They don't even like
> Homemade ice cream and cake.
> —Ruby Lee

CHAPTER 34

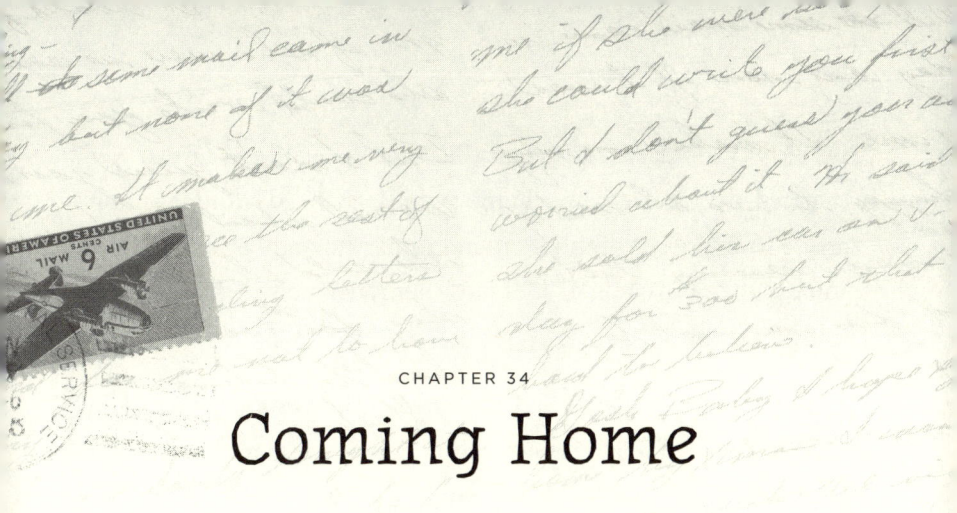

Coming Home

To live a good life takes work.

FIRST LIEUTENANT WILLIAM R. CANNON was honorably sent home to finish his tour of duty in August 1946, landing in Fort Sam Houston, Texas, in September of 1946.

He piloted two-engine C-47's and C-46's. He served as a pilot on C-46 with the 4th Combat Cargo Squadron and 322nd Troop Carrier Squadron in China. He transported cargo and military personnel to various points in China. Upon completion of this assignment, he flew to the Asiatic-Pacific Theater of Operations and was a pilot in C-46's and C-47's at Nichols Field, Luzon, for a period of eight months. Lt Cannon also Piloted military officials to Guam, Okinawa, Biak, Japan, all the Philippine Islands, and New Guinea. He was assigned to the 1st Combat Cargo and then was assigned to 512 Troop Carrier. After Dec 8th he was reassigned to 329 Carrier Squadron and then to the 322nd division.

He would tell tall tales about "flying by the seat of his pants." There were times when he lost tail wings, had to perform belly landings, and other close calls. He was taught to count to 50 on every takeoff. "If this bird isn't up by 50, it's not flying, so start praying," he'd say.

Buster went into the service as a hotshot football hero turned ego-centered flyboy. He came home with a changed attitude—more astute to the needs of those around him. Although he still retained some of the air of confidence of those hero attributes, there was something different.

He grew up. Dad developed clear goals for becoming financially independent. Although never wealthy, he was a responsible provider. We never were lacking what we would need for a full, happy life.

When I think about what is needed to live a good life, the list is really very simple, yet very complicated. To live a good life takes work. The work begins within you and continues to spread like a contagion to the people in your life.

The Cannons lived simply in nice homes that were well cared for. They didn't move up in real estate to finer houses. The house they purchased became a home to last.

Food was not gourmet or lavish. It was never wasted, and it was always delicious. Ice Cream was homemade with ice salt in a hand crank maker so we all had to take turns cranking. We learned early in childhood that it was hard work making that ice cream but the reward was high.

> **Living simply meant that you laughed.**

Cars were Plymouth's that were affordable and always purchased with cash. We never called roadside assistance for gas or a flat because Dad made sure everyone could change a tire. If you were down to a quarter of a tank of gas, then you had better go fill it up.

Family—no matter what happened in your life—was family. There would always be a disgusting Glad-Ass to make it entertaining, but you had to love him or her anyway. Everyone is a jerk once in a while. If you think too much of yourself, you will eventually be humbled.

Do unto others are not just words; they are gospel to live by. Doing good works gives you value as a person. If you don't like your life, then change it.

Finally, living simply meant that you laughed. Weird Wade made life hard for Ruby, but her laughter kept her spirit alive. I can hear all of my aunts laughing. It rings in my brain to let me know I am living a good life.

Mom and Dad still lived in that simple house when he got sick. They had their den with two rocking chairs residing in front of the TV. This is where you could find them on any given night watching their favorite shows together. There still was plenty of gossip about the show or the stars in it that could be heard during commercials.

Dad had lung cancer. I remember his words. He wasn't sad; he was going to do what it took to beat it. "I did it to myself with the cigarettes," he explained. "There is no one to blame but me. You know, I still wish I could have a cigarette though."

> His fate rested in two doctors that wrestled with each other's ego for the proper treatment.

He had a doctor and a surgeon with differing opinions. The doctor was somewhat negative; while the surgeon was absolutely sure he could remove it all.

Dad had faith in both of them because they were doctors. Doctors held more esteem than an old football hero from high school. His flyboy days long past were no bravado anymore. The hotshot zone manager was long retired. So his fate rested in two doctors that wrestled with each other's ego for the proper treatment.

The surgeon drew a picture of his cancer, where it was located, and how it would affect his lung capacity. His drawing was much like a plumber might draw showing you where your drain is clogged. He efficiently explained the procedure and in the end had Dad smiling with anticipation to have the surgery.

Dad was tough and not afraid of the pain. Now with the plan drawn out by the architect, it was time to start the project of cancer obliteration.

Surgery was welcomed with his smile showing in those blue eyes.

> Finally, his ear hair was removed, and any sign of nose hair was properly plucked.

Mom had her own prepping to do for surgery. She washed and ironed a dozen pair of pajamas, then folded them to be ready for packing. Dad was placed on his perch in the den in front of the TV with a towel around his shoulders so Mom could perform a proper haircut. Finally, his ear fuzz was removed, and any sign of nose hair was properly plucked.

The operating room was ready, and so was Dad. We all were around his bed with the room filled with nervous laughter to make us all feel more at ease. A little white cap got placed on his manicured head. With a smile on his face, the nurse rolled Dad down the hall, and he was singing, "I'll Be Seeing You." He had one hand in the air keeping time like a song leader in a band as we saw him pushed into the operating theater.

CHAPTER 35

They Got It All

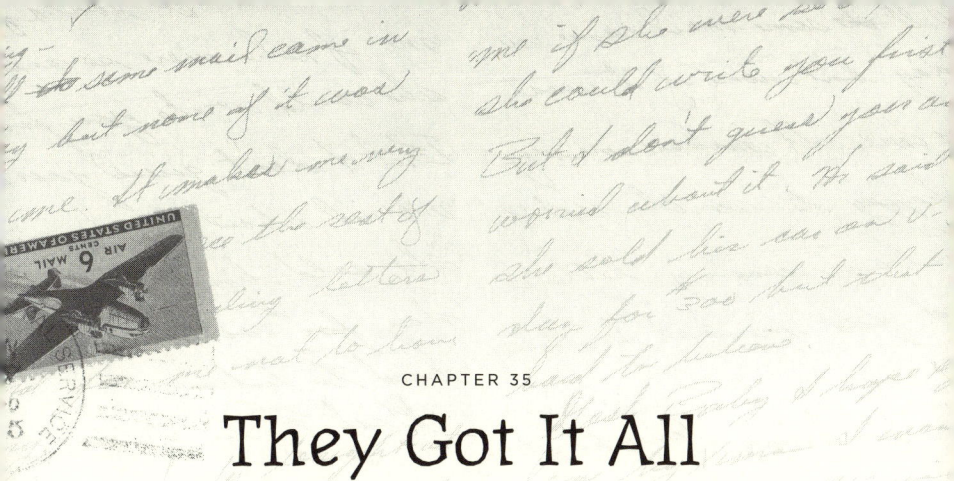

I know part of his gratitude was for himself, but he was most grateful that Mom would not have to be alone.

"Buster, good news honey, they got it all," Mom whispered in his ear. "Isn't that wonderful? The surgeon was so happy when he told me."

Dad peered out of his baby blues with a smile and fell right back asleep; peaceful that he would be there for Mom for more years.

The next day his surgeon visited with handshakes, smiles, and laughter as he described the surgery and its success. He was 99 percent sure that he indeed got all the cancer and surrounding tissue. Mom already had Dad into his fresh pressed pajamas before the surgeon arrived. Norman Rockwell could not have painted it any better. We were going to get to keep him for a long time.

> Mom already had Dad into his fresh pressed pajamas before the surgeon arrived.

After the surgeon left, Dad's primary doctor came in to join our party. We expected to see his elation, but instead, he wasn't as sure as the surgeon was about the prognosis. He wanted Dad to have radiation just in case.

Mom and Dad loved this doctor. He was old school and had been recommended by their friends as one of the best. Whatever he said was gospel. Radiation wasn't so bad; it was nothing like chemo. This was just a minor precaution.

> He was the best dressed in the hospital.

Dad was a remarkable patient—doing everything they told him to do. He ate the hospital food with low salt and only complained three times a day as they served it. Dad was the best dressed patient in the hospital. He charmed all the nurses, and they loved him. Mom and Dad were the perfect couple and the ideal love story. The nurses would often come in to find Mom snuggled up in bed with him watching their favorite TV show.

His return home to recover meant that all his friends could come and stay as long as he could stand it. Jack came and waited on her baby brother hand and foot. She was his only sister left by now. She could not have stood to lose her "Preach." She had the Cannon spirit just as Dad did—never let life keep you down, always get back up, and find something to laugh about every day.

In her high heels, she would strut to and from the kitchen with her coffee and cigarette, which killed Dad because he still wanted one. He refrained from the typical recovering addict speeches by not saying a word about her smoking.

Jack finally took her cigarettes and coffee out to the patio, which was a blessing for Dad. It also ended up blessing me. I didn't smoke—my run in at 16 crashing my car was enough. We were sitting in the shade talking as she puffed away adding memories to my life that I will never forget. I always wondered what the smokers talk about when they huddle in the corners of a building looking as if they are gang members plotting some terrible act. Sitting there with Jack was where I got all the inside scoop on family history.

Dad's recovery was going smoothly when his lungs filled with fluid and he found himself unable to breathe one day. Jack urgently called the hospital, and they took him by ambulance to the emergency room. All the family rushed down. We were afraid of what we would find.

> Why are you all here?"

Instead, we arrived to find a chipper, happy fellow, sitting up in bed with a tube draining fluid from his lung. He gave that hardy laugh. "They got me here and stuck that thing in my side. It hurt like a son of a gun, but then it felt better almost immediately. Hey, why are you all here?"

Crisis avoided, we took Dad home. He continually gave praise for those who took care of him. I know part of his gratitude was for himself, but he was most grateful that Mom would not have to be alone.

He was her world. Her housework was dutifully performed each week so they would have their nest clean. She fixed his favorite meals. Chicken fried steak, mashed potatoes, gravy, and green beans. She would get round steak and pound it out with a meat mallet until it was thin and tender. A good dusting of salt and pepper was added to each side before it was dipped into flour. Then in a cast iron skillet with hot Crisco, it was fried until crisp on both sides.

Mashed potatoes were made from real potatoes, with lots of butter and cream. These were put in the mixer and beaten until they were smooth as silk.

Green beans were cooked a good hour with bacon grease that she kept in a coffee can under the stove. This was topped off with cream gravy made by scraping all the little pieces of meat, flour, and grease from the cast iron skillet. This was browned as she added extra flour. Once it was good and brown, she added whole milk and stirred it until thickened.

This feast took an hour and a half to prepare and the same amount of time to clean up. For her, it was worth it. She would hear Dad's praise throughout the meal, "Mary, this is the best meal I have ever had. You outdid yourself this time. I don't think it can be better."

Dressed to kill including her highest heels, Jack flew back home to Oklahoma knowing Preach was in good hands, and well on the mend. We all were at peace for our hero was happy and healthy. Mom and Dad resumed going to the movies and singing.

CHAPTER 36

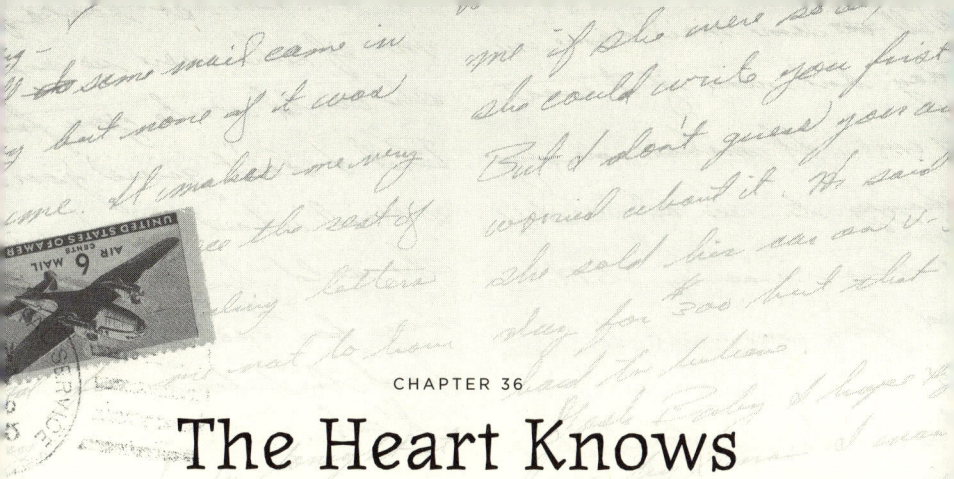

The Heart Knows

*She bought jumbo eggs and was delighted
when there was a double yolked one. When you got
a double yolked egg that day, it meant good fortune.*

DAD WAS RECOVERING NICELY, although his radiation was making him tired. However, he remained happy to be alive and with Mom.

He enjoyed breakfast and coffee with family on Saturday mornings now instead of golf. I made a point of being there because I didn't want to miss a chance to chat.

Mom didn't want help in the kitchen. She liked to do things her way at her speed, which was not fast. She picked out the best bacon at the store by looking not only through the little clear spot on the package, but she lifted up the clear spot to look under it for fat. She didn't want too much fat on the bacon.

She bought jumbo eggs and was delighted when there was a double yoked one. When you got a double yolked egg that day, it meant good fortune. She only used Rainbow white bread and real butter for toast.

The bacon was cooked slowly in the pan so it would not burn or undercook. By turning it often on low heat, every spot could be perfectly done. She would fry the eggs in the bacon grease by taking a spatula and continually splashing up the grease on top of the egg to cook both sides. The hot fat would make a bubble on top of the egg and cook the top at the same time as the bottom. This made the egg perfectly runny only in the middle.

Toast also had a special preparation. She didn't have a toaster, but a toaster oven that broiled the toast only on one side leaving the bottom soft and the top toasted. The butter got applied to the untoasted bread in specific spots. One dollop went on each corner and one in the middle. When it toasted, the butter had five gooey yummy spots with a bite of the unbuttered toasted spot.

Mom made Dad's coffee in an old coffee pot on the stove, not an electric pot. These are the ways she cared for him. If it wasn't perfect, she would start again. Dad would have eaten anything, but she wanted him to have the best.

This particular morning was different because Dad was unable to eat. He had such bad indigestion that he couldn't put a bit of food in his mouth. The radiation had upset his stomach a few times and it had made him fatigued. He wanted to sit in his chair in the den and watch a little golf.

Damn, Sam, this indigestion is terrible.

Mom and I went ahead and ate and I visited with Dad in the den as she spent the next hour and a half cleaning the kitchen. The bacon grease made a big mess. But when she was done with the stove, there would be no hint of grease anywhere.

Dad was not talking anymore, nor was he smiling. He would grunt and stand up, hunching over a bit, "Damn, Sam, this indigestion is terrible."

CHAPTER 36: The Heart Knows

I was worried that it was more than indigestion the longer it went on. I told Mom that I thought we should get him to the hospital. Then I said, "We need to take you to the hospital, Dad. Something isn't right." He refused to go.

After 30 more minutes, the pain was not subsiding and the indigestion was getting worse. Finally, he agreed. Mom helped him get out of his pajamas and into his khakis.

We should have called an ambulance. Dad had a heart attack, and he had lost muscle in his heart by waiting. He was also coughing up some blood due to the radiation.

We started calling the family again, but this time we called the Marine Corps to bring home our oldest son to be with his own "Old Dad." Dad had continued the name "Old Dad," only without the wingdings.

> It felt like Satan entering the room bringing hopelessness and despair.

He now had two doctors. He had his primary care, the one they loved, and a cardiologist. They both had different information to share.

Being the more pessimistic of the two, the primary care doctor always seemed to be the bearer of bad news every single time. I was beginning not to like him. In fact, it felt like Satan entering the room bringing hopelessness and despair.

His news of Dad's lungs not healing from the radiation was the bad news. I was angry now and did indeed see him with a tail and horns. Had it not been for him, his lungs would not have been damaged by the radiation. Not only were his lungs injured, but the stress of the radiation is most likely what brought on the heart attack.

The cardiologist was the angel appearing who brought smiles to the room and hope to all of us daily. "Buster, you are looking great today. Your blood pressure is good, and your heart damage is not severe enough to keep you from the lifestyle you are living. But we are going to keep you here while your doctor gets some healing into your lungs after the radiation." Mom rushed home to wash and iron more pajamas. She also called her sister to help. She would not be leaving the hospital so she would need her sister to take care of the house and wash. And she trusted her sister to stay with Dad when she needed to be away for a while.

No more bacon and eggs, chicken fried steak, or green beans with bacon grease. Dad was back on hospital food, but he was grateful he was alive to eat it. He smiled through each salt-less forkful. "Mmmm, this is so good. Do you want a bite?"

> Two medical problems besiege me
> I need cures without delay
> I'll send requests to Jimmy Swaggart
> And one to Tammy Faye.
> This hospital food is just so gross
> That I am forced to waste it
> Before the doctor subscribes for me
> He should be forced to taste it.
> —Ruby Lee

CHAPTER 37

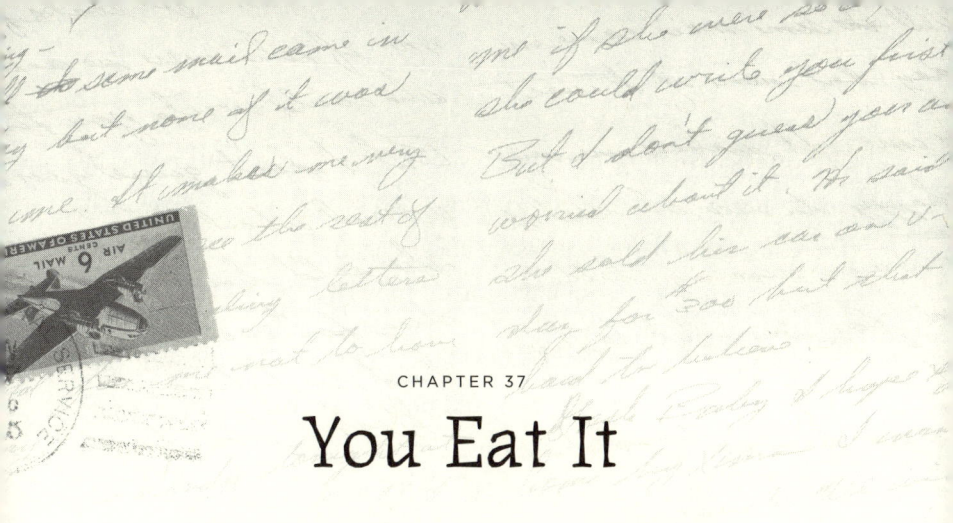

You Eat It

*I figured that if we could even get some ham grease
and salt in him, that would be better than nothing.
He had not eaten anything for five days by then.*

EVERY DAY IT WAS THE SAME. The Devil arrived with his news for the day, followed by the Angel delivering good news and hope. We liked the Angel much better. With all his glad tidings, Dad would contently try his best to heal while Mom had hope for the future.

His grandchildren visited—entertaining him with stories. Just having the oldest one there on loan from the Marine Corps was a huge morale booster.

Lucifer arrived with his news that it was time to "bring out the big guns." It was a steroid called Solu-Medrol. This heavy-duty steroid was needed to see if they could heal Dad's lungs damaged by the radiation. There was still hope for healing, and the side effects seemed minimal with heartburn being the worse, per the Devil Man.

Dad became a zombie—not sleeping, and not eating.

Solu-Medrol was Devil-spit, which brought on much more than heartburn. Dad became a zombie—not sleeping, and not eating. Each of these side effects became the focus of the family to try to eliminate.

It didn't help that the hospital served him Brussels sprouts just as he was losing his appetite. He looked down at his plate and said, "Well, hell, there are those damn half-ass cabbages again." After that, he didn't eat anything on the plate.

> **If it's that good, then you drink it."**

The hospital brought in some Ensure with vitamins and calories since Dad would not eat. He would not take one sip. Trying to encourage him, I tasted it and told him, "Dad this is not bad. Just try it. It's really good." His smile came back as he answered, "Well, I'm so glad its good. If it's that good, then you drink it."

We all loved the hamburgers at "Castles" next to the hospital. They were as good as homemade. We brought in hamburgers for him with all the things he liked on it. They cooked the meat a little crispy and applied mustard, tomatoes, pickle, onions, no cheese, and a toasted bun.

> **Please, Dad, eat just a little bite.**

It was a no-go. Dad would not take one bite. I went home and fixed one of his favorite meals. I made ham, green beans, and red potatoes cooked together in a big pot. I gave it a good dousing of salt and pepper. I figured that if we could even get some ham grease and salt in him, that would be better than nothing. He had not eaten anything for five days by then.

We put him in a wheelchair, and the entire family went down to the hospital solarium so we could do a big family meal together. It seems like all of our best times were with food. I had the nice warm pot of one of his favorite foods and had topped that off with another favorite, homemade cornbread with real butter.

Dad was happy in the solarium. He wanted to go there every day. He smiled, laughed, and found joy being there with his family until we tried to get him to eat the food. Then we heard, "No thank you." By then I was almost begging, "Please, Dad, eat just a little bite." He responded with a sweet smile, "No. No thank you."

CHAPTER 37: You Eat It   205

Another one of the nasty side effects of Solu-Medrol was that he did not sleep. He did not close his eyes nor did he sleep one wink. Dad would not stay in bed. He would not stay in his chair. And Dad was as restless as a bee on a flower. It didn't matter how many sleeping pills or meds they gave him; he just didn't sleep.

The insomnia caused a set of different problems because someone needed to be with him in the hospital at all times. Mom's sister would stay with Dad while Mom would go home and clean up for a few hours. Then Mom would stay up all day and part of the early evening with Dad. Then I had the duty at night, but I could not last more than a day or two without sleep.

Dad would wander the halls and want to go to the solarium at night. He would try to get up, and I would have to call for help. He was worse than a newborn baby because no one could catch a lick of rest. I couldn't help but doze off a few times that ended in Dad disappearing. I devised a way to tie a string to him and me, so I would wake up and know he was up again.

He had to pee all the time, and that was a chore to keep getting him up and down every hour to pee. He would not use the hospital assigned bottle to go in. He wanted out of bed, and we wanted him to stay put.

Late at night while driving to and from the hospital I would find myself bargaining with God to make Dad get better. I praised him for the time that we had with Dad but begged for more time to spend with him. Mom's prayers were silent and unanswered ... just like mine.

Dad's prayers were with the chaplain who was the only person with the guts enough to

> Dad chose one time for repentance after the chaplain had left.

ask him if he wanted to pray. I can't figure out why it is so hard to pray with someone out loud. What has our voice so confined that we cannot enunciate words out loud to the God who made us? Dad welcomed the prayer, which was not for healing, it was for peace and strength. His prayer was for praise and to console those around him.

Dad chose one time for repentance after the chaplain had left. He gathered around his grandchildren for a time of cleansing. He confessed about the Indian arrowheads. There was amazement in their eyes as they heard the real story, and realized the magic Dad had provided in their lives.

He continued to cleanse with laughter naming all of the games where he had cheated so he could win. Then he told of the ones he purposely lost. Then he addressed his oldest grandson, a Marine, to tell him how proud he was of him, and saving a big hug for the youngest grandson. He didn't know at that time that the youngest would follow in his footsteps.

Dad's body was starting to fail him. Our prayers of healing would go unanswered. The Devil and the Angel agreed. "Buster, you're going to die."

> ### "My Prayer"
> I don't want to live so long
> That they are glad when I am gone
> A burden I don't want to be
> To those who are so dear to me.
> When my time comes, please make it quick
> I don't want to be old and sick
> I'm not afraid to die, you know
> Just so long as it isn't slow.
>
> —Ruby Lee

CHAPTER 38

Hurry

Those who are born can never die;
they are always part of you.
—Bill "Buster" Cannon

I REMEMBER THAT MOMENT. Dad did not cry. He did not get angry, and he was not in denial. Dad was ready. He was tired of fighting. His lungs simply would not heal from the radiation, and his heart was too weak to continue.

He could see clearly now that he was not going to heal. He stepped out of himself to think of others, Mom, and his grandchildren. He didn't want to leave them hurting. He accepted his fate because he could not change it.

I think back to the letter in the beginning when he told Mom,

> "Darling, I can't begin to tell you how brave you were this morning. I'm so glad you didn't break down and cry because I would have, too. Nothing has ever hurt me so much as leaving home and leaving you this morning. I know I'll cry tonight but I don't care."

Mom was brave this day too as Dad ordered his "strong box" with all his papers in it. We went over each one again as he sat cross-legged on the bed. He looked at his family standing around him. "I have no regrets, not one. So I need to know if you have anything you need to say. I want your blessing and to tell me that it is OK if we just do this."

The regret was that we were going to have to say goodbye. All the bargaining and pleading was for naught. Dad reminded us that "Those who are born can never die; they are always part of you." Dry-eyed he sat up and patted us all and announced, "Well, then, let's get this on and get it done." He set upon his new job of dying.

He took all work seriously whether he was mowing the lawn, or selling a car. His motto was whatever you do in life, do it with all your might. He said, "If I am going to clean toilets, then they are going to be the cleanest damn toilets you ever saw." He took to dying with the same passion.

Ruby had belonged to the Hemlock Society to end her life with dignity and compassion. Dad didn't need the Hemlock for help. He had a nurse with orders to give him the maximum dosage of Morphine as often as the laws would allow. The shots started now.

With his hair clean and face shaved, he dressed in his freshly ironed pajamas. His first supply of Morphine was administered as he laid down to start his new task. Still able to talk he comforted Mom, he chatted with her about their life together. The memories and how they never missed an opportunity for happiness. The family was more important than friends, yet friends managed to intertwine with his family.

> **He caught his last football and piloted his last trip.**

The shots came on time, one after another until Dad slipped into a restful sleep. Mom did not need to wait any longer for he could not hear her so she wept with wailing now. She didn't need to be brave; she just needed him to stay. There was no other voice, no other sounds, just the inconsolable wailing with her clawing at his bed, his sheets wadded into her fists.

The Morphine kept coming into the rhythm with her tears. Dad slipping further and further away. As the nurse came into the room, she could hear him say, "Hurry, hurry." She didn't realize that he was not talking to her, but to God.

We begged Mom to please tell Dad that it was OK to go. "Please, Mom, he needs to know that you are OK with him leaving now. Don't make him stay any longer."

Her face contorted with more agonizing tears until she could catch a breath to speak, "Buster, it's OK to go, honey. I don't want to let you go. You have been my world, my love; you are the best part of me. It is OK to go. You go now. It is OK. You go now."

Dad's eyes never opened, and we heard his one last whisper, "Hurry," to which God granted his plea, and Dad was gone.

Now in the dark, dark night, we saw him peaceful. No more was he struggling under the Morphine to breath. There was only the uncanny stillness of peace.

He caught his last football and piloted his final flight. He lived his life as the pilot of his own aircraft. Dad was responsible for the destinations in his life, and for teaching me how to fly on my own.

Last Will and Testament

I won't have a lot of cash
To leave you when I go
Or worldly goods that you could keep
Or stocks and bonds that grow
I bequeath to all of you my love
My greatest gift is laughter
Remember therefore with a smile
And let the tears come after
But with the tears-and make them few
Just think of me with pleasure
For the happy times that we have known
Have been to me—my treasure

For all of those who've gone before
And all of whom remain
Made my life fulfilled with love
That's all I want of fame.
The End
—Ruby Lee Carter Cannon

CHAPTER 39

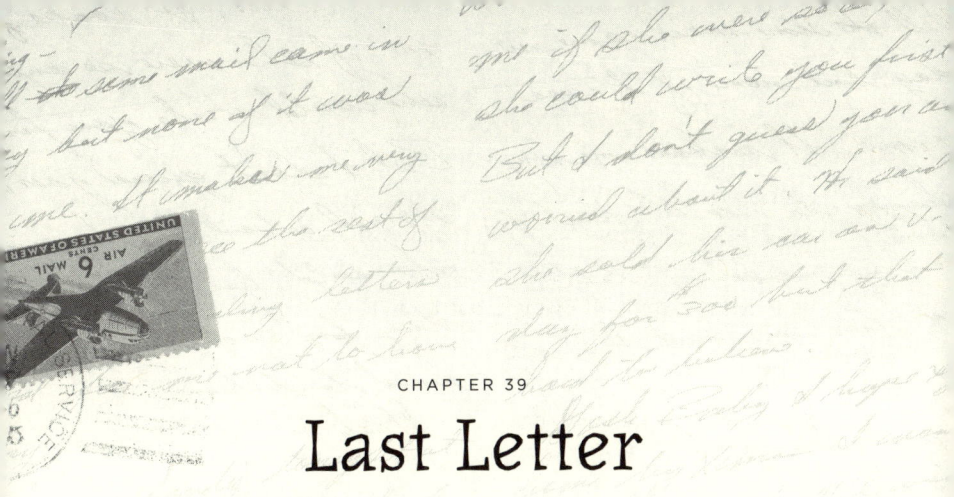

Last Letter

*You can tell me about who has done what and when,
but most of all we can talk about love and our life together.
That is what we both are interested in.
We will be wonderfully happy.*

July 1946

Hello Darling

We were in Tacloban and then we flew to Del Monte in time for lunch. Then we had dinner with the Philippine Army. It was very good. For meat, we had pork, fish, and some kind of fowl. Then we had potatoes, tomatoes, green onions, a native salad, and a fruit salad in a pineapple shell. It was not only good to look at but it was wonderful to eat.

We left there and went to Zamboanga. I flew through some of the roughest instrument weather that I have ever been in. It tossed the airplane around like a ball.

Darling I would like so very much for you to see some of these places, they are beautiful and the Filipinos are wonderful people.

We will have a lot to talk about when I get home.

The nearest I can figure we should have 3,277.50 in August when I get home. That is unless you spend some before I get home next month.

I got a Shawnee newspaper in the mail but no letters. I read every word of it even the ads and the fillers, and boy I sure enjoyed it. It would sure help things a lot if they would ever straighten out this mail service.

I had a piece of fresh peach pie with ice cream on it this afternoon. It was sure good. I guess you will be glad to see me no matter how much I weigh, but I don't want to get fat before I see you.

Honey I'm glad you are going to have a nice little home for me to come home to. Darling you have everything all ready for me, but don't you dare lift anything that would hurt you.

We will have a lot to talk about when I get home. I'll tell you about everything when I get back, and there is a lot to tell you. Then you can tell me about who has done what and when, but most of all we can talk about love and our life together. That is what we both are interested in. We will be wonderfully happy.

Your love always

Bill

Darling stop writing will be home about 1 Aug will call upon arrival Anxiously = Bill

CHAPTER 39: Last Letter   213

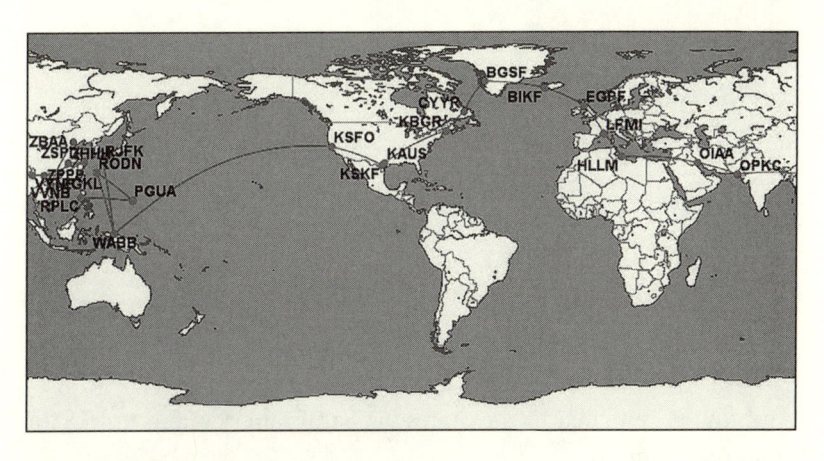

Dad's Flight Path beginning

Bergstrom Air Force Base: Austin, Texas

Godfrey Army Airfield (later named Dow Air Base): Bangor, Maine

Goose Bay Air Base: Labrador

Sondrestrom Air Base: Greenland

Naval Air Station: Keflavik, Iceland

Scotland

Istres-Le Tube' Air Base: Marseille, France

Wheelus Air Base: Tripoli, Libya

Abu Air Base: Cairo, Egypt

Abadan Air Base: Abadan, Iran

Karachi, Pakistan

Nampong Airfield: Myitkyina, Burma

Liuzhou, China

Shanghai, China

Kunming Air Base: China

Back to Shanghai

Hankow, China (Hankau)

Hanoi, China

Peiping, China

Then on to Manila, Philippines

Guam

Okinawa

Biak

Japan

New Guinea

And finally returned to the States via San Francisco and onto Sam Houston Air Base.

CHAPTER 39: Last Letter 215

216 Buster the Football Flyboy

Afterword

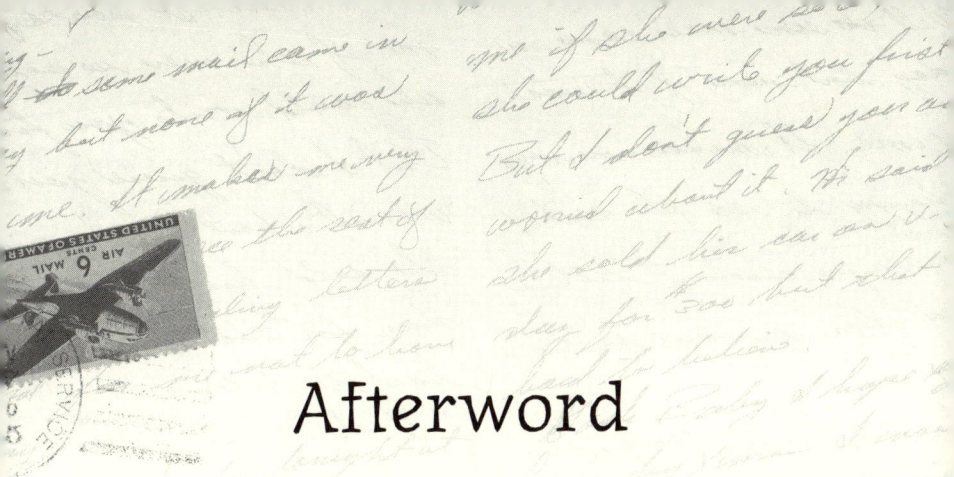

AND, THEY WERE WONDERFULLY HAPPY ... and created an expansion of friendship and happiness within and outside of the family.

You don't know how or who will come into your life that can change it. What footprints are out there that we will find, and whose will we follow?

God used a self-centered, middle-class football flyboy to touch so many people in his life. He ended his life with the grace that increased the well-being of others that knew him.

Buster's grandsons prove to be his biggest fans, following in his footsteps. Their goal is to imitate the man who was their hero. Both boys raised on horseback know a thing or two about horses too.

David the oldest served his country in the Marine Corps. He continues Dad's heritage by providing moments of intrigue with his three boys by hiding arrowheads and cheating at games.

Following the flyboy, Steve, the youngest fought for his country in Iraq, witnessing the tragic faces of death. He brought home that baggage expressed in a poem he wrote graphically describing the bomb that killed some of his fellow Marines.

His rhymes filled the first stanza of vision blurred by dust storms and faulty equipment. Then the poem ended with the IED that destroyed his friends as he pulled their truck through the rubble. His heart on paper, written eloquently in cadence described what changes our warriors' lives.

Steve keeps following the flyboy by receiving his pilot's license to reach the skies that Dad found in such wonder.

Both can feel Dad's soul in a church in a time of quiet, and Sunday dinners with family. They need to reconstruct habits that build our families, keeping us connected whether we deserve it or not.

Our family includes the Glad-Asses because they are family. We have learned to forgive the grandparent for spoiling children, or giving them hot fudge Sundays at midnight.

Flyboy has taught our family to keep soaring and changing our views to be better people. Yes, we were and are wonderfully happy.

— Lisa Cannon Reinicke

Cannon Recipes

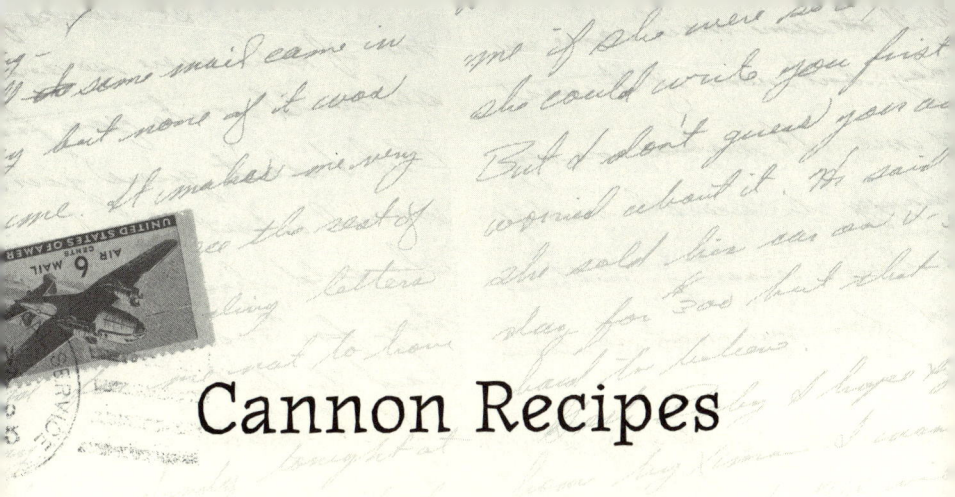

Cleo's Ironed Grilled Cheese Sandwich
—David Baugh (Jack's grandson)

Sourdough bread (has to be sourdough)
Sharp Cheddar Cheese (big hunks of it. No kraft slices)
Butter
Aluminum foil
Iron

Spread butter smoothly on the inside of the sourdough bread.

Place the sandwich in foil.

Heat up an iron on high (steam works better).

Then iron the hell out of it until the cheese melts.

I miss that ole girl making those for me—it was the best!

Grandma's Donuts

    1 cup sugar
    4 tsp baking powder
    1 tsp salt
    ¼ tsp cinnamon
    2 eggs
    1 cup milk (got to use whole milk not that watered down crap)
    1 tsp vanilla
    2T oleo (That is margarine, renamed Country Crock and many other brands now.)
    4½ cups of flour (without weevils, please)
    Oil for frying (Crisco is the best)

Mix sugar, baking powder, salt, and cinnamon. Add eggs, milk, vanilla, and melted Oleo. Beat well. Add 3 cups of the flour. Mix well and then add the other cup. Cover and chill for an hour.

The dough should be soft and sticky, but firm. If necessary add a little more flour. Grandma winged it.

Working half of the dough at a time roll out about ½ inch thick. You need to flour your work space and rolling pin to keep the dough from sticking to it. Using a donut cutter, cut out donuts.

If you don't have a donut cutter you can use a biscuit cutter. For the hole you can use the top of a martini shaker. Then make yourself a sip of Vodka while you have the shaker out.

Heat enough oil in a fry pan for about 2 inches of hot oil.

When hot gently drop in the dough. Flip when golden brown. Douse those babies good with sugar when you take them out of the oil.

Now get everybody out of the way so you can get the first one!

Candied Sweet Pickles-Canned

Ms. Cannon for Gaines

    2 gallons of pickling cucumbers (Grown in garden is best.)
    2 cups of pickling salt
    1 gallon of boiling water
    1 T Alum
    5 cups of white vinegar
    8 cups of sugar
    ¼ cup of pickling spice
    1T celery seed
    1T mustard seed

Cut cucumbers into cubes about 1-inch pieces.

Put cucumbers in a pickling crock. No metal, glass or stone. Add salt and boiling water.

Cool and cover with a dish towel for 1 week. If mold forms remove the mold with a spatula.

On Day 8 drain the water. Boil another gallon of water and pour over cucumbers in the crock. Cool and cover.

On Day 9, repeat day 8 only add the Alum.

On Day 10, drain. Do not add water, instead boil vinegar, sugar, and spices and add to the crock.

On Day 11 drain but save all the juice and reboil it and add back in.

On Days 12 and 13 repeat Day 11.

On Day 14 put cucumbers and mariande in jars. Seal with a hot water bath.

Sounds like a lot of trouble. Trust me... It is worth it...

Mom's Toast
(We call it Mimi toast now)

> White bread
> Aluminum foil or cookie sheet
> Real butter (not the spread, a cube of butter)

Line up the white bread on foil or a cookie sheet.

Slice 3 thin pats of butter. Divide the pats into approximately thirds. Put a piece of butter on each corner of the bread and one in the middle. Place cookie sheet under broiler or in a toaster oven broiler.

Watch carefully. As the butter starts to melt, the bread in between the butter will start to brown. You toast only the top of the bread, not both sides.

You don't need jelly. I promise.

Ham, Green Beans, and New Red Potatoes

> 2 ham hocks with bone (or a leftover ham bone from a ham dinner, that makes the best)
> salt and pepper to taste
> 1 pound of fresh green beans
> 1 Onion, chopped
> 1 pound of new red potatoes

Put the ham in a large pot and fill with water. Add lots of salt and pepper (gotta get that sodium intake up there). Now boil the hell out of it until the meat falls off the bone.

Remove the bone and add your trimmed green beans and chopped onion. Add water if you need to. Simmer for 40 minutes then add the new red potatoes and simmer until they are done.

Grandma's Biscuits

This isn't hard but worth it.

> Crisco shortening
> 2 cups flour (without weevils)
> 1 tsp baking powder
> Pinch of salt
> 1 cup buttermilk
> ½ tsp baking soda

In a bowl, place an egg-size of Crisco shortening. (Grandma really didn't measure all of this, she guessed.)

Sift the flour, baking powder, and salt together. (I know unheard of these days, but do it.)

In a separate bowl mix the buttermilk and baking soda.

Add the buttermilk and baking soda to the flour mixture and combine with a fork. The fork will get all gooey, keep mixing.

Turn the dough out onto a lightly floured surface and knead for 30 seconds.

Roll out about ¾ inch thick. Be sure to flour your rolling pin.

Cut out with a biscuit cutter. Bake for 425° F for 12 to 15 minutes

Whatever you do, don't slap anyone away from the table if they say "Biscuits again!"

224

Other books by Lisa Reinicke

Arnold
The Cute Little Pig with *Personality*
Lisa Reinicke

DAVID'S CHRISTMAS WISH
Lisa Reinicke
Illustrated by Scot McDonald

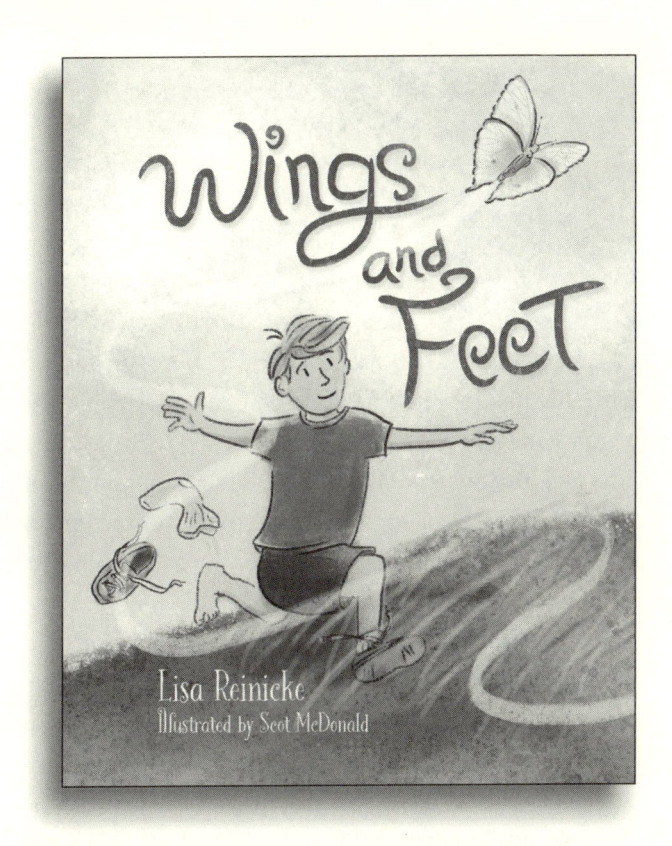

Wings and Feet

Lisa Reinicke
Illustrated by Scot McDonald

Bart's Escape Out the Gate

Lisa Reinicke
Illustrated by Analise Black

Lisa Reinicke, is the founder and CEO of Automotive Warranty Network. She owes the company success to her dad—the *Football Flyboy*—for instilling priceless life lessons. His methods taught her early on to never give up, do the right thing, and be creative in leadership. Lisa serves on several board of directors for companies helping to direct cash flow and maintain high company policy and high standards in a desire to help other achieve success.

She is the majority holder of Our House Publications and author of four published children's picture books and other non-fiction books. Lisa was honored with the Mom's Choice Gold Award for lifetime literary excellence for her children's book Wings and Feet.

Lisa is an avid a storyteller and author of 35 children's stories that have appeared throughout Colorado on local TV shows, elementary schools, and bookstores. The stories have been published in 3 collective recordings for distribution for A Goodnight Sleep Company.

She passionately works raising money for charities that improve children's lives physically, emotionally, and spiritually. With a strong military background dating back to the original colonists, through the Civil War, WWI, WWII, and her sons veterans of Iraq; she works passionately for charities supporting our military veterans. Her father, Buster the Flyboy, ingrained the moto: "The more you have, the more you give," into her fabric.

Calling Colorado her home, Lisa loves spending time with family, but doesn't sit still for long. She finds time for hiking, snowshoeing, traveling, knitting, sewing, and crafting with her five grandchildren.

To connect with Lisa please visit her website at *www.LisaReinicke.com/contact/* and join her on Facebook and Twitter.

www.LisaReinicke.com

lisareinickeauthor/

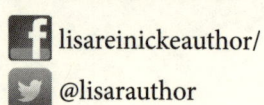

@lisarauthor